Three Moments of Love
in
LEONARD COHEN
and
BRUCE COCKBURN

For my father
whose dream of paradise,
despite appearances,
is not that different from mine.

Three Moments of Love

in

LEONARD COHEN

and

BRUCE COCKBURN

Paul Nonnekes

Montreal/New York/London

Black Rose Books No. DD291
Hardcover ISBN: 1-55164-177-1 (bound) Paperback ISBN: 1-55164-176-3 (pbk.)

Canadian Cataloguing in Publication Data
Nonnekes, Paul, 1961-
Three moments of love in Leonard Cohen and Bruce Cockburn

Includes bibliographical references and index.
Hardcover ISBN: 1-55164-177-1 (bound) Paperback ISBN: 1-55164-176-3 (pbk.)
1. Cohen, Leonard, 1934- —Criticism and interpretation.
2. Cockburn, Bruce, 1945- —Criticism and interpretation. I. Title.
Ml400.N814 2000   782.42164'092'271   C00-900456-4

Grateful acknowledgment is extended to the following for permission to reprint copyright material: to McClelland & Stewart, Inc., for excepts from *Beautiful Losers* and from *Stranger Music: Selected Poems and Songs,* © Leonard Cohen; and to Golden Mountain Music Corp., © for all songs by Bruce Cockburn.

Cover design by Associés libres, Montréal

C.P. 1258	2250 Military Road	99 Wallis Road
Succ. Place du Parc	Tonawanda, NY	London, E9 5LN
Montréal, H2W 2R3	14150	England
Canada	USA	UK

To order books in North America:
(phone) 1-800-565-9523 (fax) 1-800-221-9985
In Europe: (phone) London 44 (0)20 8986-4854 (fax) 44 (0)20 8533-5821

Our Web Site address: http://www.web.net/blackrosebooks

A publication of the Institute of Policy Alternatives of Montréal (IPAM)

Printed in Canada

Table
Of Contents

Acknowledgments...vi

Introduction: Two Subjects—I and S.......................................1

Part One: Leonard Cohen—Three Moments of I

First Moment: Symbolic Machinery......................................15

Second Moment: Veiled Feminine...25

Third Moment: Feminine Angel...36

Part Two: Bruce Cockburn—Three Moments of S

First Moment: Loving Father..51

Second Moment: Troubled Son..92

Third Moment: Big Circumstance...146

Conclusion: I and S Apart, Together......................................173

Index...180

Acknowledgments

Writing is often a lonely task, one that brings both a distinct kind of monastic pleasure, but also the burdens that come with reentry into the world of the everyday. Much of this work was written in the summer of 1998. I want to thank my family: my wife Tania, and my two children, Cammi and Amos, for enduring with good spirit my sometimes melancholic writing moods. I want to especially thank Tania, friend, lover and colleague, who has been both consistently encouraging of this project, at the same time as its most incisive critic.

Thanks also must go to two of my colleagues at Red Deer College, Nancy Batty, and James Martens, who generously read and commented on early versions of the manuscript. Also, thanks to all my colleagues in my department at the College, who have sustained an environment of interdisciplinary curiosity that has given me the encouragement and the freedom to pursue my critical dreams. And, lastly, thanks to Linda Barton and Dimitri Roussopoulos, of Black Rose Books, for their support of this project.

Introduction

Two Subjects—I and S

This study engages in a series of reflections on the work of Leonard Cohen and Bruce Cockburn, two Canadian singer-songwriter-poets. Although it may, at first glance, seem odd that these two artists, who are so different in style and temperament, are brought together in one work, they were selected because of the way in which they both engage the question of love in relation to the identity of the subject. From the base of their work, two subjects are proposed, I and S. The subject I is drawn from Cohen's work and the subject S is drawn from Cockburn's work. This study explores the desire of I and S, specifically, the masculine desire of I and S, as both of these subjects, in their own distinctive way, yearn and search for love.

Leonard Cohen has gained status as an international pop icon representing a dark and mysterious masculine sexuality.[1] In popular culture he is probably best known for his music, from

1

Songs of Leonard Cohen,[2] in 1960 to *The Future*[3] in 1990. Yet, in the literary world, he had already in the 1960's established, before the popular reception of his music, a reputation as a talented poet with such works as *The Spice-Box of Earth*[4] and *Flowers for Hitler*,[5] as well as an innovative novelist with the publication of *The Favourite Game*[6] and *Beautiful Losers*.[7]

The intent of this book is not to exhaustively analyze the breadth and diversity of Cohen's work from the 60's to the present. Nor does this book attempt to make connections between Cohen's art and his life. Rather, my intent is to examine the images of masculine desire that Cohen's work presents through the construction of an ideal subject. Inspiration for the construction of this ideal subject is found in the work of the French psychoanalyst Jacques Lacan,[8] but also the work of the German critical theorist Walter Benjamin.[9] Yet, the section on Cohen that constructs this ideal subject does not attempt to systematically connect the work of Cohen to the work of Lacan and Benjamin, but attempts to construct a subject who embodies the style expressed in the work of Cohen, as well as the work of these two theorists.

This question of style is important and speaks to what may strike the reader as an imbalance in this book in the treatment of Cohen and Cockburn-the section on Cohen is about a third the length of the section on Cockburn. Cohen's style is dense; every metaphor is a concentration of sentiments which crosses over to the reader or listener and explodes, producing the displacements of metonymy. It is in this way that his style is like Lacan's, who privileged metonymy and who created his famous knots, and also like Benjamin's, who loved the fragment and expressed himself in now-times of meaning. On the basis of this apprehension, the three moments in the Cohen section are written as a series of concentrated interpretations that, it is hoped, will lead the attentive reader to multiple associations. Along stylistic lines, and in keeping with Lacan, the task is not to employ the discourse of the master, providing systematic interpretations in the position of "the one who knows," but to employ the discourse of the analyst, providing provocative interpretive statements that incite the desire of the other.

Thus, in my treatment of Cohen, the decision was made not to be exhaustive and systematic, but to be selective of those fragments that seemed to point to an ideal subject. For this task, the decision was made to first concentrate on the 1960's novel, *Beautiful Losers*. In that novel, two principal characters called F and I emerge, and the novel weaves around the friendship between F and I. I is, for Cohen, the ultimate loser, but yet, as the novel unfolds, we realize that it is precisely his status as loser that allows I to become the ideal subject. I's link to Lacan can be usefully interpreted as an allegiance to an ideal centered on the subject's encounter with nothingness, with an always-already ruined original. Desire must move beyond the illusions of ego security that bind one to particular material structures in order to arrive at the position of enlightenment.

This book presents the subject I as a subject who achieves enlightenment through three moments. The use of three moments reflects a dialectical sensibility, a desire to express movement in thought and expression which captures conflict and struggle, as well as the attempt to reconcile, in some fashion, the conflict and the struggle. The first two moments of I are ones that unfold in the novel *Beautiful Losers*. In Lacanian terms, the first moment is when the imaginary ego of I is destroyed by the symbolic work of F, everything from exploding fire-cones, to body-building, to the famous Danish Vibrator. Yet, F's symbolic work harbours its own illusions, illusions that are based in the pretensions of phallic power, and the second moment is therefore needed in which I as loser, especially in his encounter with the love of the saint-goddess Catherine Tekakwitha, overcomes phallic symbolic illusions and arrives at an encounter with what Lacanians call the real, a moment of love defined by nothingness and absence.

This is as far as *Beautiful Losers* goes in the path of enlightenment. What is proposed in this book is that a third moment develops for I (based in Cohen's work in the 80's and 90's, and even though Cohen no longer uses the name I), which is based on the relationship between the masculine subject I and the feminine angel. The construction of this third moment in the masculine desire of I receives inspiration from the work of Walter Benjamin, especially Benjamin's abiding devotion to a form of Judaic mysticism. Again, this book does not attempt a systematic appraisal of the connections between the distinctive forms of Judaic mysticism in Cohen and Benjamin. Rather, the task is a stylistic one concerning the coming together of sentiments that inform the experience of I. In this context, the third moment of I is one that returns the masculine subject I to the mundane social-material world in a way that is fundamentally different from both the symbolic destruction of the first moment of love and the distanced indifference of the second moment of love. And this unique and distinctive return to the mundane social-material world is defined by the encounter the masculine subject has with the feminine other represented in the figure of the angel.

Bruce Cockburn has been most defined by his music, yet the development of social, political and economic themes in that music has worked in tandem with a consistent and active support for international issues of social justice, from the resistance to dictatorship in Central and Latin America, to the struggle against landmines in Africa.[10] Cockburn is probably best known in Canada, but has built a strong following in the United States and Great Britain, as well as continental Europe, especially the Netherlands and Germany.

Cockburn's musical career took off in 1970 with the release of his first album, *Bruce Cockburn*[11] which was soon followed in 1971 with a second album, *High Winds, White Sky*.[12] Both of these albums reflect a pastoral mood, a celebration of a peaceful, reflective country way of life that is in harmony with nature. With *Sunwheel Dance*[13] in 1972 Cockburn's work begins to engage in a spiritual quest within the context of a celebration of nature. *Salt, Sun and Time*[14] in 1974, *Joy Will Find a Way*[15] in 1975, and *In the Falling Dark*[16] in 1976, and *Dancing in the Dragon's Jaws*[17] in 1979, all speak to the movement of that spiritual quest in a Christian direction.

The 1980's was a decade where Cockburn articulates in his music an increasing concern with issues of social justice, especially on the international scene. *Humans*[18] in 1980, *Inner City Front*[19] in 1982, *The Trouble With Normal*[20] in 1983, *Stealing Fire*,[21] in 1984, and *World of Wonders*[22] in 1986, all reflect this theme. Especially important for the latter two albums was Cockburn's touring of Central America, his horror over the atrocities committed there by right-wing dictatorships and his deep support for and commitment to the Nicaraguan revolution.

The release of *Big Circumstance*[23] in 1988 marks a third phase in Cockburn's music, which moves through 1991's *Nothing But a Burning Light*,[24] 1994's *Dart to the Heart*,[25] and most dramatically, in 1997's *Charity of Night*.[26] Although he continues to sing about social injustice, his lyrics begin to articulate a higher degree of suspicion about the possibilities of creating paradise within the present circumstances of life.

The second section of this book engages in an exploration of Bruce Cockburn's vision of masculine desire, concentrating on the lyrics in his music. As was the case with Cohen, there is no attempt in this section to make connections between Cockburn's lyrics and his life. Rather, this section involves itself in the construction of an ideal subject that seems to be suggested by Cockburn's lyrics. And, again, it is all about style. Cockburn's style is not that of Cohen's concentrated image, but that of the journal or travelogue, involving a continuous production of experiential observations that reflect a distinctive journey through life. This speaks to why the section on Cockburn needs to be so much longer than the section on Cohen. It produces an extended commentary that, in parallel to the lyrics, develops an ongoing narrative of the ideal subject.

While paralleling the lyrics of Cockburn, the construction of this second ideal subject is inspired by the work of the French psychoanalytic feminist, Julia Kristeva.[27] As with the section on Cohen, the section on Cockburn does not attempt to systematically connect the work of Cockburn to the work of

Kristeva, but attempts to construct an ideal subject who embodies the style expressed in the work of both Cockburn and Kristeva.

The section based on Cockburn's lyrics constructs an ideal subject called S. The reason for selecting the letter S is to contrast it with a designation, common for Lacanians: the use of Ş, the so-called barred subject, the subject that has no authentic origin, but is always-already lost.

As in the section on Cohen's I, the experience of Cockburn's S can be usefully divided into three moments. Again, as was the case with Cohen, the use of three moments is motivated by a desire to express a dialectical movement in the subject S that captures conflict and struggle as well as the attempt at resolution. Yet, while I's three moments of love express a Lacanian and Benjaminian style, S's three moments of love can be understood to express a style inspired by the work of Kristeva. And, just as the style of I is influenced by Benjamin's Judaic mysticism, so the style of S is influenced by Kristeva's Christian mysticism. The Christian mysticism of S expresses a belief that the beginnings of life-creation, birth-are fundamentally good, embody an ideal world that calls out for expression within material life, not just in the private world of meaning that exists in isolation from the world, but within the context of intersubjective relations that are social, political and economic in expression. Rather than arrive at the awareness of the nothingness that grounds all existence, as is the case with I, the quest of S's masculine desire is to both find expression for that which always-already good (not always-already ruined) but also, and this is very important, to critique all those expressions which do not measure up to the image of paradise that was there in the beginning.

The first moment of the masculine desire of S, expressed in the lyrics from Bruce Cockburn through to *Dancing in the Dragon's Jaws* is one that expresses for masculine desire a relationship with what we may call, inspired by Kristeva, the "loving father."[28] This is a relationship, strongly mediated through natural images of sun, wind, and sea, that establishes an ideal parent for S that is a mother-father combination. But, as an expression in the beginning, it speaks to S's child-like apprehension of the good and the ideal that is unencumbered by the complications of the social-material world.

The second moment of the masculine desire of S is grounded in the lyrics from *Humans to World of Wonders* and speaks to the condition of the "troubled son." This is where the desire of the son moves out of the comfortable, child-like world of nature and country-side and encounters the pain of the world in a dramatic way, worldly expressions that cry out how much the social, political and economic arrangements of the world do not embody the ideal, are far from paradise. Yet, S feels the pain only in relation to the absence of the ideal, not a pure absence or nothingness, but the extent to which that which could be, namely, paradise, is not here, yet should be. And at the same time as experiencing rage at the destruction of the ideal, S also recognizes that, despite all the horror, there remains the core of love.

The third moment of the masculine desire of S, called "big circumstance," is expressed in Cockburn's work from *Big Circumstance to Charity of Night*. Now, here is the curious twist. The third moment of I based in Cohen's work moved the subject away from the indifference of an outlook bound to symbolic projects toward one that engages with the social-material world through the mystical figure of the feminine angel. S's third moment moves in a different direction than I, but given the distinctive starting-points of I and S, can be understood to arrive at a similar position. This is surprising, given that the style and temperament of Cohen and Cockburn's work are so radically different. The unifying image, in both the third moment of I and the third moment of S, is that of love. In his third moment of love, expressed most dramatically in *Charity of Night,* S realizes, much as I did, that symbolic projects of redemption can so easily become illusions that trap the spirit, and that redemptive love comes through instantaneous transformative moments that continue to motivate the subject to action in support of the ideal, while all the while realizing that any action cannot fully express the ideal.

Concerning the construction of both I and S, some questions arise which this book would like to address. How, for I and S, does masculine desire express itself? What is their relationship to the other of desire, who captivates and fascinates them? And in identification with the other, what means of expression unfolds, what forms of signification arise, what kind of poetics? How does the poetics of I and S relate to the ideal, desire's search for the primary, the significant, that which is fundamentally good? What obstacles do I and S face in their search for a relationship with an ideal other, what kind of struggle do they each face as they search for love?

How does the love sought by I and S relate to the influence of the maternal and the paternal? Is the maternal an illusory trap for masculine desire in its quest for love? Or is the maternal a necessary ground for the active expression of masculine desire in its search for love? In what way does the influence of the maternal frame I and S's access to the other and the ideal? As for the paternal, is the paternal influence needed in order to rescue masculine desire from the illusory traps of the maternal? Or does the paternal carry on the work of the maternal at another level? Is the paternal simply another mode of the maternal? Given one path or the other, how does the paternal then influence the relationship both I and S establish with the other and the ideal?

And what is the status of the feminine other for masculine desire, for both I and S? How do both I and S meet the feminine other? What is the influence of the feminine other on their being granted or not being granted love? What kind of masculine desire emerges for I and S because of the particular relationship they each establish with the feminine other?

In terms of space, what type of container is poetically constructed for the fate of love and desire? Is it small or large, protective or abandoning? Are its borders tight and thick, or loose and thin? Is the container constrictive for the active subject or expansive for the active subject? And what exactly is the relationship between the construction of the container and the passive and active modes of the subject?

In relation to time, what is the state of the beginning? Is the beginning fundamentally good, the ideal base from which desire searches for love? Or is the beginning already ruined, a lack of that which is ideal, which the quest for love will need to come to grips with? In what sense does the later build on the beginning? Is the later an active building up of the good, or is the later a continuation of active ruination?

And what about the social material world? What is the connection between the love attained by I and S and the fate of justice? How does the desire of I and S for the other's love find or not find expression in the world of economic and political ties? Does the quest for love allow for a critical position on the social material world, one where justice can be named as that which allows love, and injustice named as that which prohibits love? This brings into play the question of evil. Does evil exist, can it be named and fought against from the perspective of love, or is the consciousness of evil in the form of economic and political injustice an illusion, a trap for desire, a moment to be overcome in order to reach the higher moment of enlightenment?

NOTES

1. For an excellent guide to Cohen's life and work up until 1996, see Ira B. Nadel. *A Life of Leonard Cohen*. Random House of Canada, 1996.

2. *Songs of Leonard Cohen*. Columbia CL 2733, 1968.

3. *The Future*. Columbia-Sony CK 53226, 1992.

4. *The Spice-Box of Earth*. Toronto: McLelland and Stewart, 1961.

5. *Flowers for Hitler*. Toronto: McLelland and Stewart, 1964.

6. *The Favourite Game*. New York: Viking Press, 1963; Toronto: McLelland and Stewart, 1970.

7. *Beautiful Losers*. Toronto: McLelland and Stewart, 1966.

8. See in particular the essays in *Ecrits: A Selection*. Trans. Alan Sheridan. New York: Norton, 1977.

9. See in particular the essays in *Illuminations*. Ed. Hannah Arendt. Trans. Harry Zorn. New York: Schocken Books, 1969.

10. For a useful chronology of Cockburn's musical career up until 1991, see William Ruhlman. "A Burning Light and All the Rest," *Goldmine*. April 3, 1992.

11. *Bruce Cockburn*. True North TN-1 (Can), Epic 03812 (US, erroneously titled *True North*), 1970.

12. *High Winds, White Sky.* True North TN-3 (Can), 1971.

13. *Sunwheel Dance.* True North TN-7 (Can), Epic 31768 (US), 1972.

14. *Salt, Sun and Time.* True North TN-16 (Can), 1974.

15. *Joy Will Find a Way.* True North TN-23 (Can), 1975.

16. *In the Falling Dark.* True North TN-26 (Can), Island 9463 (US), 1976.

17. *Dancing in the Dragon's Jaws.* True North TN-37 (Can), Millenium/RCA 7747 (US), 1979.

18. *Humans.* True North TN-42 (Can), Millenium/RCA 7752 (US), 1980.

19. *Inner City Front.* True North TN-47 (Can), Millenium/RCA 7761 (US), 1981.

20. *The Trouble With Normal.* True North TN-53 (Can), Gold Mountain 3283 (US), 1983.

21. *Stealing Fire.* True North TN-57 (Can), Gold Mountain 80012 (US), 1984.

22. *World of Wonders.* True North TN-66 (Can), Gold Mountain 5772 (US), 1986.

23. *Big Circumstance.* True North TN-70 (Can), Gold Castle 71320 (US), 1988.

24. *Nothing But a Burning Light.* True North TN-77 (Can), Columbia CK 47983 (US), 1991.

25. *Dart to the Heart.* True North TN-82 (Can), Columbia CK 53831 (US), 1994.

26. *Charity of Night* True North TN-150 (Can), Rykodisc 10366 (US), 1997.

27. See in particular the essays in *Tales of Love.* Trans. Leon S. Roudiex. New York: Columbia UP, 1987.

28. The term "loving father" is comparable to Kristeva's "imaginary father" as it appears in "Freud and Love: Treatment and Its Discontents," *Tales of Love.*

PART ONE

LEONARD COHEN
THREE MOMENTS OF I

Like a bird on the wire, I have tried in my way to be free.

First Moment:

Symbolic Machinery

In the beginning, we find I, our subject, in a series of intense encounters with his friend F and F's "ordinary eternal machinery," a machinery which conceives of the body as a multiple symbolic generator, continually pumping out desire in the most eccentric ways.[1]

As in the "Telephone Dance" with F and Edith, where F says "I became a telephone" and "Edith was the electronic conversation that went through me."[2] A profusion of production occurs with F imploring I, in his usual didactic manner, to "connect nothing."

The problem is I connects everything, weaving his imaginary thread through all forms, bringing them into the whole, under the lure of maternal love. F's task is to be the big daddy phallus, symbolic destroyer of imaginary wholeness, cutter of connecting threads. F implores our subject to empty his memory, to listen to the present. There is a deep friendship between I and F, one not surprising given the incredible force of attraction between I's imaginary quest for wholeness and F's destructive symbolic activity.

The difference between them, yet their mutuality, is shown in the work of the bowels: I is continually constipated, can't let go, and is thereby marked with an incredible loneliness; whereas, F is always losing control of his bowels, always spilling himself out for the world. F is going to teach I something about this.

I is "weighted with a sealed bowel" and unlike F's spilling he cannot "help the flowers and the dung beetles."[3] Thanks to F, though, he is seeking a way out: "Please make me empty, if I'm empty then I can receive, if I can receive it means it comes from somewhere outside of me, if it comes from outside of me then I am not alone."[4]

The problem I has is a familiar one for a masculine desire that is consumed with the maternal connection, a connection that nurtures narcissism. The warm and cozy love the maternal once provided locks I into a fantasy world of the one true love. As I says, "I am the sealed, dead, impervious museum of my appetite. This is the brutal solitude of constipation."[5]

F's training of I is an education in hysteria. I tells us that "he was ready to use any damn method to make me hysterical."[6] F once said that "hysteria is my classroom."[7] This is said on the occasion of F giving I a prayer box with the inscription: "A man translates himself into a child asking for all there is in a language he has barely mastered."[8] We all know the inadequacy of language in the face of the real. The question is what will be the response to this condition. F's solution is that of the poet's: "the notion that he is not bound to the world as given, that he can escape from the painful arrangement of things as they are."[9] And now, as the master and teacher, he must convince I that to gain some access to the real requires an hysterical language that is not bound to this world and its "painful arrangement." A special symbolic *jouissance* will destroy all arrangements that have settled in and become frozen like idols, fetishistic illusions, imaginary solutions as a longing for security.

F's hysterical solution arrives in the form of a box of fireworks. I plays with the "red and green fire cone" and with the "skyrocket"[10] and finds his imaginary ego coming apart. Once bound, I's secure ego becomes unbound, unraveled. This is a painful process for I, and as he experiences the pain of the explosions he cries out for "nummy, nummy,"[11] longing for the maternal retreat. No retreat is possible now, though, and the dummy ego of I "has sneaked out into the furniture."[12] The exploding symbolic fireworks of F are unplugging the previously sealed orifices of I. "I've leaked all over the kitchen," says I. Somebody needs to "put me back in my skin."[13]

I faces here the inevitability of aggression in the destruction of his imaginary world. This is an aggression towards himself, a violence that turns against his constipated ego, a primary masochism that battles his narcissism in its fixation on the maternal. We have in F's explosive teaching the expression of the death drive and through its expression the possible coming-into-being of I as subject against the constraints of his imaginary ego. Why else such a fascination with dismemberment and excrement?

The explosion of F's fireworks is closely connected to sexual explosions. The firecracker and the phallus: they both blow up in your hand. F is an expert at finding new spaces to spill himself to the world. On their way to Ottawa where F will take up his position as a new Member of Parliament, F begins to masturbate while driving. I is awed at F's phallic power, which is the power of the symbolic. "I've never seen you so big," says I. "Can I hold it…I love you power. Teach me everything."[14] I claims he cannot bear his loneliness any longer and starts to masturbate with F, "two swelling pricks pointed at eternity."[15] F is able to come and enjoy his release, but I doesn't, because just before he is about to, they run into a wall, "made of a scrim of painted silk."[16] F asks: "How about the second just before you were about to shoot. Did you sense the emptiness? Did you get the freedom?"[17] I didn't for he feared the wall. F tells I that he should have kept going and disregarded the wall. There was nothing he could have done about the wall anyway, so you might as well get a good come out of it. But I cannot empty himself, cannot gain the freedom. There is always the wall for him, which has now become internalized. F wants him to forget the wall. The wall is not so dangerous. In fact, it is made of silk. It is beautiful, feminine, an aid to your pleasure.

Like the goddesses in the music group Gavin Gate and the Goddesses. I listens to them on the radio as the group makes full use of their "ordinary eternal machinery." Their electronic instruments put forth an "incessant regular sex pumping" and "electronic pulse breathing."[18] Gavin identifies with the goddesses painful sexuality and they are led into a military-like frenzy of sado-masochistic desire. They "whip themselves with electric braids."[19]

F's eccentric experimentation with "ordinary eternal machinery" is aided by the variety of instruments available in popular culture. Popular culture products, in their diffuseness, serve as one way of breaking through the imaginary wholeness, the ego isolation.

The Danish Vibrator is one of these popular culture instruments. Edith cannot make herself come any more. F, naturally, has the symbolic solution and is going to design things so that Edith will "perfect the pan-orgasmic body"[20] First, says F, "we do it with books." F reads from books, everything from "What We Can Learn From the Anteater" to "Auto-Eroticism in Windows."[21] This gets Edith excited. F reads of "unusual sex practices" where "there is some greater pleasure than orgasm through intercourse."[22] He reads of "bizarre practices" that "involve a measure of mutilation, shock, voyeurism, pain and torture."[23]

There is pleasure here in the death-drive. That pleasure comes through the destruction of the usual and the courting of the unusual and the bizarre. F continues to read, the practices becoming even more bizarre and shocking: "Men masturbated to death. Cannibalism during foreplay. Skull Coition."[24]

During this symbolic enactment, Edith "moaned in terrible hunger."[25] She desires to "be freed from the unbearable coils of secular pleasure."[26] Secular pleasure involves coils that keep us bound to the cult of the here and now, the everyday. We desire to "soar into the blind realm," lose our attachments to petty material pleasures, find the pleasure "so like sleep, so like death," a pleasure that is "beyond pleasure."[27]

Books provide for a symbolic destruction, destroying the imaginary ego, the bound ego, a space where unusual desires can be expressed. Secular pleasure involves a reduction of excitement in the homoeostatic quest of the imaginary ego. The symbolic language of sado-masochism blasts apart that boundedness, no longer reducing excitement, but allowing the subject to be overwhelmed by *jouissance*.

Books, however, are not enough in this symbolic quest. The technology needs to be more powerful. Enter the Danish Vibrator, which like the Telephone Dance, is part of F's ordinary eternal machinery. F plugs in the D.V. "A degrading spectacle followed."[28] As it should, according to the demands of the death-drive. Edith gets hold of the D.V. and it "hummed like a whistler as it rose and fell over Edith's young contours."[29] With the assistance of the D.V. both Edith and F are able to come. Thinking they are finished, they pull the plug on the D.V.

The D.V. stops, but then begins to "produce a shattering sonic whistle."[30] Says F: "It's learned to feed itself."[31] F and Edith realize that we do not control the ordinary eternal machinery. We are its servants as it makes light of our puny egos and shows whose boss. The death drive rules.

The D.V. moves toward Edith. She is frightened but then "numbed by horror and the prospect of disgusting thrills, she was ready to submit."[32] Here, we have gone beyond the pleasure principle, and in this state Edith submits totally to the death work of the master D.V. She then becomes "nothing but a buffet of juice, flesh, excrement, muscles, to serve its appetite."[33] The coherence is lost, the boundedness provided by ego work abandoned, the victory is to symbolic destruction.

The work of symbolic death through popular technology continues with the Charles Axis body building. F gets his extraordinary body by responding to an advertisement on the back of a comic book.[34] The ad has seven frames which show men bullied because they are too skinny, they get muscles, are no longer bullied, and then get the women. The story line is, of course, so formulaic, but yet, as far as F is concerned, it has its usefulness. Both F and I are too fat, and F has decided he is going to lose his fat. He works out with the Charles Axis method, and by treating it as a religious experience, is able quite quickly to lose the fat he despised. But at this point a disturbance is registered in F's discourse, a disturbance that will deepen as things progress. After doing the popular symbolic body work, F is bullied by Charles Axis who castigates him for being too skinny. Men constantly chase after the phallic ideal, where work is never ending in the quest for symbolic solutions. From F's perspective, this is surely an advance over I's passivity, signified by a lonely sedentary lifestyle where fat is the result. In fact, I confesses that he "didn't listen to Charles Axis."[35] All he had to do was give up fifteen minutes a day to achieve a half-decent body. To F, I has an "arrogant body."[36] I wants to be "Blue Beetle," "Captain Marvel," "Plastic Man," not Robin but Batman, "Superman who was never Clark Kent."[37] I goes on to admit that he "wanted miracles," that he "wanted to wake up suddenly with X-Ray vision."[38] These are all fantasies of easy completeness, womb quests, imaginary solutions, desire without any struggle, ecstasy without any contact with the heavy handed work of material symbols, plenitude without the experience of difference. But the symbolic quest of F has its own difficulties for I. In the mad quest to get beyond imaginary entrapment in the maternal F loses the insight that there is a lack at the very core of his being and that the task is to somehow accept the nothingness of that space, that he is inherently incomplete, that once fat is done away with, skinny is there to make its demands. The insight of lack is avoided by both imaginary and symbolic solutions, or, as we shall see, can only be grasped through a mutual destruction.

It turns out that the real problem for I is not just imaginary entrapment, which seals him in the grasp of the maternal, the great mother, but also symbolic entrapment, spun out into the world in a dance of signs, always moving forward impatiently, yet never satisfied. A response to this problem begins to emerge in the collision between native spirituality and the spirituality of the Christian missionaries. In fact, the Telephone Dance must be an ancient ritual, for we find the French Catholic missionaries trying to stamp it out among the Mohawks elders of Kahnawake. The elders do not connect things the way the missionaries want. The missionary says, "You won't be able to hear me if you keep your fingers in your ears."[39] Instead, dribble and spit comes out of the elders mouths. For the missionaries, the continuance of the Telephone Dance will lead the natives into hell, where a demon will "cut off your head, extract your heart, lick up your brain, drink your blood, eat your flesh, and nibble your bones."[40] In a sense, the Telephone Dance is played out by the missionaries themselves, but now under the sign of repression. There is a sado-masochistic pleasure for the missionaries in meticulously describing the torture, the return of the repressed.

The collision intensifies in the encounter between a Catholic priest and Catherine Tekakwitha's uncle.[41] Catherine's uncle stays true to the Indian ways, but the priest persists in trying to covert him to Christianity, especially the Christian conception of heaven. In the priest's vision, heaven is a place where all differences are reconciled. It is a beyond of unitary wholeness in stark contrast to the pain of division which pervades our sinful lives as material beings. For Catherine's uncle, heaven does not overcome the divisions. Death connects you with your ancestors and your relatives around the fire. But first you must begin an arduous journey in which you will have to overcome many obstacles. Once you have done that, the most important event to happen, in order for you to achieve true redemption, is to have your brain removed from your skull. This was the key to the Telephone Dance: the connection made between the fingers was made possible by the absence between the ears. Subjectivity is an absence, a fundamental lack in being, a nothingness which is filled and then emptied, filled and then emptied. The journey of becoming brainless is itself the key where the puny brainy ego is removed and spirit is the emptiness left. This means that true spirit is not a beyond that we are blocked access to, but is the essence of what is the here and now; it is nothing.

NOTES

1. Interpretation of the first two moments of I is inspired by Lacan, and more specifically, two works on or influenced by Lacan: Richard Boothby. *Death and Desire: Psychoanalytic Theory in Lacan's Return to Freud.* New York: Routledge, 1991, and Slavoj Zizek. *The Sublime Object of Ideology.* London: Verso, 1989.
2. Leonard Cohen. *Beautiful Losers.* Toronto: McLelland and Stewart, 1966, p. 35.
3. Ibid, p. 41.
4. Ibid, p. 41.
5. Ibid, p. 42.
6. Ibid, p. 59.
7. Ibid, p. 59.

8. Ibid, p. 59.
9. Ibid, p. 59.
10. Ibid, p. 67.
11. Ibid, p. 67.
12. Ibid, p. 68.
13. Ibid, p. 68.
14. Ibid, p. 97.
15. Ibid, p. 97.
16. Ibid, p. 97.
17. Ibid, p. 100.
18. Ibid, p. 78.
19. Ibid, p. 81.
20. Ibid, p. 178.
21. Ibid, p. 179.
22. Ibid, p. 179.
23. Ibid, p. 180.
24. Ibid, p. 184.
25. Ibid, p. 184.
26. Ibid, p. 184.
27. Ibid, p. 184.
28. Ibid, p. 185.
29. Ibid, p. 188.
30. Ibid, p. 190.
31. Ibid, p. 190.
32. Ibid, p. 191.
33. Ibid, p. 191.
34. Ibid, p. 73.
35. Ibid, p. 122.
36. Ibid, p. 123.
37. Ibid, p. 123.
38. Ibid, p. 124.
39. Ibid, p. 86.
40. Ibid, p. 86.
41. Ibid, pp. 119-121.

Second Moment:

Veiled Feminine

F in his quest for symbolic destruction of I's imaginary world, does not understand this idea of spirit as emptiness or nothingness. And it should not surprise us that the key for the redemption of masculine desire for both I and F should come through an experience with the feminine. I experiences imaginary entrapment because he is caught up in his first love, which was earlier referred to as an experience of the great mother. F sees it as his duty as a friend, teacher, and master to destroy that attachment between I and the maternal mother. F's work is phallic, coming in between I and the maternal to send I out into the world of "ordinary eternal machinery." The destruction of I's imaginary commitment was important, but definitely not the end of the story, for F's symbolic world is itself in need of destruction, needs to be shorn of its phallic pretensions toward control and mastery, the lure of systems. So, even though I has experienced the fall from grace, separation from the maternal, his very connection with the maternal opens the possibility for redemption at another level, now not at the level of the imaginary great mother but at the level of the great goddess, that wonderfully ecstatic experience of the maternal beyond all imaginary and symbolic forms. Thus, masculine desire must escape the maternal at one level, through the work of F's phallic symbolic, but must return to the maternal at a new level of experience, that which approaches the real. Masculine desire is always ever drawn to the maternal, our first and only love. The question is whether that love consumes masculine desire and leaves it forever speechless and lonely, or whether masculine desire can experience that love anew from the perspective of ecstasy.

That new experience of ecstasy begins to take form in the relationship between I and Catherine Tekakwitha. There is a special attraction between I and Catherine, given that Catherine has been made a saint by the Jesuits. This leads I to think about what F meant when he said that I needed to go down on a saint in order to cure his loneliness. F says that "[a] saint is someone who has achieved a remote human possibility."[1] That "remote human possibility" is something that F cannot attain, because it "has something to do with the energy of love."[2]

The energy of love so important for ecstasy is only possible now through the work of the feminine saint. It is the love of the Goddess. Contact with the love energy of the saint-Goddess brings about "a balance in the chaos of existence," a balance that does not "dissolve the chaos"[3] but gathers the chaos in to calmly embrace its passionate fury.

The love energy of the saint-goddess reigns in the impatient movement of male desire, expressed in the work of the symbolic phallus. I tells us that there is "something warlike and arrogant in the notion of a man setting the universe in order."[4]

When male desire is able to embrace the love energy of saint-goddess the movement is not a regressive one, but a new movement forward. Embraced by saintly love, the eccentric movements of masculine desire are gently encouraged to come together in moments of wonderment.

Chaos is here embraced in a moment where it is lovingly captured. So embraced, the male "rides the drifts like an escaped ski. His course is a caress of the hill. His track is a drawing of the snow in a moment of its particular arrangement with wind and rock."[5]

I learns these things, however slowly. Witness his first love-making with Edith. He allows himself to linger on her thigh. "Then it was just a shape," says I, "and for a blessed second truly I was not alone, I was part of a family."[6]

The love energy of Catherine Tekakwitha comes through in her baptism by the Jesuit priests into the family of Catholicism.[7] The water of baptism establishes Catherine's connection with the father, the phallic line of paternity. A disturbance is registered in this phallic line, though, when Catherine spills her glass of wine, and the red wine spreads everywhere. There is thus a contagion effect to the love energy put out by Catherine the saint-goddess. The paternal line of baptism by water turns suddenly into the wine of love, no longer contained within the symbolic rite. Through the contagion effect, the red wine love spreads and spreads, exploding the boundaries of paternal security.

We know that Christ turned water into wine. This was, as well, an outpouring of wine-love to the world. In connection with Catherine's outpouring of wine-love to the world, we discover the son's connection to the mother, not to the symbolic father. There is a baptism here, into mother-son love, as in Mary's love for Christ.

Catherine embodies feminine maternal love. And her wine of love spreads to I. I is Catherine's son. She is there to lead I away from F's symbolic destruction to a higher *jouissance* only allowed to a masculine desire that is embraced by the saint-goddess.

I tells us that Catherine's baptism is "apocalyptic" with apocalyptic meaning "that which is revealed when a woman's veil is lifted."[8] Men are veiled from the real, not by the father, the paternal, but by the mother , the maternal. Up until this point, I has been fully in the imaginary through his love connection to the maternal. He has been consumed by fantasies of completeness, fantasies that brought loneliness and not redemption. I's narcissism has now become a problem. I has ended up trapped in a world of sameness, a world always ever self-generated, going nowhere, lonely, boring.

If I is to lift the veil, he needs to encounter with the feminine as nothingness. Nothingness as love, a love that does not leave us constipated and lonely, a love that spreads and spreads, opening up our desire. This is a love that will lie outside the enclosure, a love that does not trap us in another system, like F's.

I meets the veiled woman at a political demonstration with F.[9] The crowd at the demonstration is connecting, becoming consumed by the rhetoric of Quebecois nationalism, the illusory language of wholeness and completeness established through blood as fetish. As this is happening, however, I connects with a woman in the crowd who is behind him, whom he cannot see. She is veiled, which is incredibly exciting to I. She grabs him and I's blood begins to flow. The blood is also flowing amongst the demonstrators as they protest against the terrible English, and the attempt by the English to destroy the French Quebecois blood connection. They shout, "give us back our blood" which is "our nourishment and our destiny…the builder of the body the source of the spirit of the race…our ancestral heritage…the undercurrent which they can never divert."[10] This is blood as a unitary quest, the unity of the people, spreading through the crowd, connecting them in a common purpose, absorbing F and I as well.

Yet, the blood that seeks unity does not achieve its goal and, moreover, I does not meet the woman where his blood can find its release. In fact, the crowd disperses with nothing really accomplished. The quest for unity ends up with nothing and I cannot find the woman—she is still veiled—and has not come. "F, I cried, I didn't come. I failed again."[11] F realizes that something more important has been achieved. He responds: "No, darling, you passed."[12]

I is passing and F is failing. This is especially important with respect to the feminine. F says, "I have followed women everywhere…I followed them and I sank down with them."[13] The veiled woman is a problem for F, because she lures masculine desire away from a *jouissance* that, although multiple, follows a straight and linear path.

F tells us that his problem with women is that they "hissed at me."[14] This hissing of women is, for F, oh so different from the comforting sounds males make. Males go "Shhh…Shhh and the roots are raised against the storm. Shhh, the forests are cleared so the wind [hiss] will not rattle the trees."[15] The hope of F is that the hissing of women's desire is unable to rattle the phallic tree.

The hissing of women is associated in F's mind with animal desire. Poor F is tormented with the wild sounds of animals and women. He cries out: "Will the animals stop howling, please."[16] Stop the women—hiss—stop the animal desire.

F loves dances, but not foreign dances. "I love dances that have rules, my rules."[17] F loves rules. He is constantly using the ruler, drawing his lines, straight across the page. Rules are a form of symbolic security that allows F to court diverse expressions, but within a circumscribed area. In order to hear "the Voice" masculine desire, armed with symbolic machinery, "labored, plowed, muzzled, fenced."[18]

Sorry F, your symbolic project is failing. The voice that leads comes from elsewhere. "The voice comes out of the whirlwind."[19] It is a product of the feminine Hiss.

F's particular masculine style is madness. He has been able to get past I's imaginary unities through madness. F says of I that, "You were the wall which I, bat-like, bounced my screams off, so I might have direction in this long nocturnal flight."[20] We find master F fleeing the wholeness through mad flight.

At the same time, F is deeply discontented and disturbed with his style. And in his perplexity he realizes that he would really like to be like I. I is "the good animal [F] wanted to be."[21] F is realizing the failure of symbolic madness as a response to the problems of imaginary security. Curiously enough, this leaves revealing possibilities for I the student of F, who was for so long learning to overcome imaginary maternal security, but now moves to another plane of insight. I, unlike F, is able to connect with the feminine, and more specifically, with Catherine's desire, is able to achieve forgetfulness and the realization that there is Nothing beyond the veil.

The problem is F "cannot stop teaching."[22] Is there not a fundamental problem with symbolic eccentricity? Does it not circle back continually? Does masculine desire need Catherine's indifference? Does it need a connection with nothing? F has "nothing but a system."[23] whereas I is "bound by old laws of suffering and obscurity."[24] F fears these traits of I; he is "fearful of the cripple's wisdom."[25] F, you were never tormented, you never suffered, never trembled before the terrors. I has and F understands the connection with redemption: "Has loneliness led you into ecstacy."[26]

F and I are bonded. F says: "Our love will never die."[27] His letter to I arises out of this love, "like sparks from dueling swords."[28] There is both excitement and tension in the bond established between two differing masculine desires. Centered on the mystery, chasing after the mysterious essence, the feminine. The feminine, though, is veiled. And as veiled is the source of masculine desire as ever restless, chasing, pursuing.

"Magic is alive."[29] Magic "rests in an empty palm. It spawns in an empty mind."[30] It is only when the subject is emptied that he can experience magic. Did F neglect to properly empty himself? Will this be left to I?

F recalls I's tale of how Indians look at death. There was a bark hut beside the path. There lived Oscotarach, the Head-Piercer. "It was his function to remove the brains from the skulls of all who went by, as a necessary preparation for immortality."[31] Spirit is only a skull. Subjectivity is emptiness. Is this the lesson for I in the tree-house? F says, "Perhaps the tree-house where you suffer is the hut of Oscotarach."[32] I's first lesson: subjectivity is not imaginary wholeness. I's second lesson: subjectivity is not F's symbolic systems, F's ordinary eternal machinery. I must lose his brain and catch hold of the emptiness that is the real. "The moonlight wants to get in your skull. The sparkling alleys of the icy sky want to stream through your eye-holes."[33]

F recognizes his problem: "We who cannot dwell in the Clear Light; we must deal with symbols."[34] Poor F, his symbolic work was needed in the beginning. He was a hard master, destroying I's puny ego. This was an important task, setting the scene for redemption, the emptiness, the skull without the brain. But now he is no longer needed. F cannot enter the tree-house, like I. It is "too lonely for me."[35] Instead, F "has to apply himself to politics."[36]

F is always in symbols, always remaining in symbols. This is redemption as symbolic madness, a ceaseless, movement along the chain, a phallic movement forward, never resting, always searching for new machinery, whatever works. Screw the English, blow up the Queen's statue, always resist, always turn to political agitation.

I goes beyond F through contact with the real, by realizing the importance of the feminine. The feminine is nothing. It is the veil itself. There is nothing beyond or behind the veil. All our troubled pursuits are nothing. In I's experience, masculine desire experiences feminine *jouissance*. His desire is going beyond the maternal fantasy of wholeness, beyond the great mother, his first love. But his desire is also going beyond F's phallic signifiers, past

F's symbolic machinery. Those signifiers are too pretentious, that machinery is too pompous. They all must be destroyed.

And then the maternal returns for I. Not as wholeness, great mother. The maternal returns as a great goddess, as Mary, mother of Christ. I is Christ, with Mary now his wife.

The return of the maternal occurs through identification with the experience of Catherine Tekakwitha. I's access to the real occurs through Catherine, through her self-torture and death. She was the ultimate loser. And I is a loser like Catherine.

Catherine asked: "What do you think is the most horrible painful thing."[37] And then she proceeds to enact it. She built a fire and "spent several slow hours caressing her pathetic legs with hot coals."[38] She "branded herself a slave to Jesus."[39] Which was Catherine's link to Mary.

I's devotion to Catherine is like the devotion paid to Mary in the Catholic tradition. It is a devotion that brings about an irruption of the maternal, which wreaks havoc with the symbolic tradition. Catherine's love for Jesus was like Mary's, mother to son. I being a loser understands this. There is a maternal connection where the child signifies pain, the pain of separation. This is a pain that is experienced by those, like Catherine and I who identify with the maternal. Catherine was able to get past the pain, not by fixing it, but by experiencing it, and then going beyond it.

Catherine said: "My Jesus, I have to take chances with you."[40] Jesus is here both son and lover. And in bonding to her son-lover, Catherine experienced the most painful, and yet most ecstatic, love. Through pain comes death, death of the subject. As I, in identification with the experience of Catherine, passes through this pain, this death, he is bound to suffer. Yet, by suffering he is able to attain the real. The real is not a beyond achieved by going beyond pain and suffering. In pain and suffering, in defiance of F's symbolic confidence, I is in the real, the real as nothing.

Catherine, in line with Mary, gives herself up for I, for masculine desire. I was a young boy, a dreamer, caught up in the imaginary. F's big phallus led him away. Yet, it is I in his loneliness that Catherine loves. Here, the maternal connection is still strong. Catherine goes through death, achieves ecstasy, so that I can achieve ecstasy. She "formally offered her body to the Savior and His Mother."[41]

Catherine is losing and I is listening. I then descends from his lonely tree-house. Through F's symbolic machinery, he has moved past oneness. Through Catherine's suffering, he has moved back toward oneness. Oneness as nothing and ecstasy.

NOTES

1. Leonard Cohen. *Beautiful Losers*, p. 101.
2. Ibid, p. 101.
3. Ibid, p. 101.
4. Ibid, p. 101.
5. Ibid, p. 101.
6. Ibid, p. 101.
7. Ibid, p. 102-105.
8. Ibid, p. 105.
9. Ibid, pp. 125-131.
10. Ibid, p. 129.
11. Ibid, p. 131.
12. Ibid, p. 131.

13. Ibid, p. 157.
14. Ibid, p. 157.
15. Ibid, p. 157.
16. Ibid, p. 157.
17. Ibid, p. 157.
18. Ibid, p. 158.
19. Ibid, p. 158.
20. Ibid, p. 161.
21. Ibid, p. 161.
22. Ibid, p. 161.
23. Ibid, p. 162.
24. Ibid, p. 163.
25. Ibid, p. 163.
26. Ibid, pp. 163, 164.
27. Ibid, p. 164.
28. Ibid, p. 164.
29. Ibid, p. 167.
30. Ibid, p. 168.
31. Ibid, p. 168.
32. Ibid, p. 196.
33. Ibid, p, 196.
34. Ibid, p. 197.
35. Ibid, p. 196.
36. Ibid, p. 196.
37. Ibid, p. 206.
38. Ibid, p. 206.
39. Ibid, p. 206.
40. Ibid, p. 211.
41. Ibid, p. 214.

Third Moment:

Feminine Angel

Having passed through the ordinary eternal machinery and the veiled presence of the feminine, I believes that he should not try and patch up the gnawing hole in his desire.[1] He now has no interest in staying firmly on course in an ultimate chase after his mirror reflection, one where he discovers harmony with a feminine other who is the object of his desire. Rather, he wishes to escape the gaze of mutuality that is believed by many to be the obligation of every good subject.

I mocks his friend F's well-worn masculine desire which longed for power over the feminine other. I tells us how F's days as a lady's man came to an end:

His muscles were numbered and his style was obsolete.[2]

Everything F prized about his desire was lost to a fire that consumed:

And all his virtues burning in this smoky holocaust.[3]

Believing that he was master, convinced that he had the power to preach, the feminine other called F down from his lofty heights of hubris to teach him something different:

> *Now the master of this landscape, he was standing at the view*
> *with a sparrow of St. Francis, that he was preaching to.*
> *She beckoned to the sentry, of his high religious mood.*
> *She said, "I'll make a space between my legs,*
> *I'll teach you solitude."*[4]

In trying to woo the feminine other, and subsequently control and master the feminine other, F, as a lady's man, offered her what he believed to be his sexual potency, narcissistically enhanced through a multiple mirroring, offered her protection for what he believed to be her essence: her birth-giving capacity:

> *He offered her an orgy, in a many-mirrored room;*
> *he promised her protection, for the issue of her womb.*[5]

Yet, the feminine other spurned these offers, was not at all impressed by these attempts to woo her, and announced the real future for masculine desire:

> *She said, "The art of longing's over*
> *and it's never coming back."*[6]

As a lady's man, F, however, was a slow learner, slow in the process of becoming other, becoming feminine, understanding nothing:

> *The last time that I saw him, he was trying hard to get*
> *a woman's education*
> *but he's not a woman yet.*[7]

Watching F's death as a lady's man, I comes to the conclusion that it would be a good idea to stop writing romantic love poems, poems that tried to convince everyone who heard or read them, that his masculine desire was in harmony with the feminine reception of that desire. Especially those poems about roses. I has this to say about roses:

> *I was never bothered by roses.*
> *Some people talk about it all the time.*
> *It fades, it blooms.*
> *They see it in visions, they have it, they miss it.*
> *I made some small efforts to worry about the rose*
> *but they never amounted to much.*
> *I don't think you should do these things to a flower.*
> *They don't exist anyhow.*
> *The garden doesn't exist either.*
> *Believe me, these things stand in the way.*[8]

Instead of the romantic moment of harmony with the other, I now believes that he needs to focus his attention, and thus his desire, on the feminine body as it has been refashioned in capitalist production, as it has become a commodity. As a commodity, the feminine body has lost the poetic aura which masculine desire surrounds it with. I thinks he needs to listen carefully to the prostitute-slave who announces the destruction of beauty and, along with this, the relationship between masculine desire and the poetic ego.

> *She reserves a special contempt for the slaves of beauty*
> *She lets them watch her die.*[9]

I will now actively participate in blasting apart the mythic spell that is woven for us by those experts on freedom and love, those who would lead us to believe that all of this talk of mutuality is progress. This is what I has to say to those who pursue this project:

> *One of these days*
> *you will be the object*
> *of the contempt of slaves.*
> *Then you will not talk so easily*
> *about our freedom and our love.*
> *Then you will refrain*
> *from offering us your solutions.*[10]

If he can blast himself out of this continuum of progress then he might be allowed access to enlightenment, not the through the illusions of self-made, authentic identity, not through the plenitude of meaning that comes from non-distorted communication with the other, but through loss, absence and death.

The destruction of auratic feminine beauty and the descent of the feminine into the swirling world of commodities is intimately caught up with the death of I's desire. In the age of high capitalism, feminine bodies have now become articles of mass consumption, staged bodies, reborn through make-up and fashion, pure artifice. As in I's experience of the bracelet and his mocking tribute to beauty:

> *She wears silver bracelets. One on each wrist.*
> *Even if she goes away I will say to myself I have not been denied*
> *the full measure of beauty.*[11]

I is here imagining a certain kind of violence, a poetic disfigurement of the feminine body. The feminine body has lost its aura for I. The feminine body has been transformed into a life-less body, a body of death, becoming petrified, stone-like. Through this movement, I's desire is rendered impotent. This represents a movement in I from the imaginary phallus, all ego and cocksure of its wooing power, to the symbolic phallus, all anxious and uncertain. And, in the last instance, it represents the death of I's masculine desire:

> *You are a dead man*
> *Writing me a letter*
> *Your sunglasses are beside you*
> *on the square table*
> *on the green felt*
> *You write carefully*
> *sentence after sentence*
> *to make your meaning clear*
> *The meaning is that you are dead*
> *dead with hope*
> *dead with spring*
> *dead with the blurred hummingbird*
> *dead with the longing*
> *to shine again*
> *in details of the past.* [12]

I is referring here to the insistence of the letter, written now by a dead man, a man who is dead to both imaginary and symbolic illusions. We witness the coming-into-being of I as subject through a unique kind of historical memory, one driven by the death-drive, where the subject emerges dead with hope, and is reduced to an endless repetition of sentence after sentence, all the same, all recalling the horror of the past and the utter futility of human efforts to conquer the horror.

For I, this dead hope, this unflinching recognition of horror, applies as well to the future. The future announces not the redemption of all that exists, not the imaginary or symbolic creation of a material-social paradise, but a persistent, continual and ever-present violence:

> I've seen the future, brother:
> it is murder. [13]

And it is the path of imaginary and symbolic control that continues to be the path masculine desire finds the most pleasurable, however lonely and isolated, however absent of contact with the other:

> Give me back my broken night
> my mirrored room,
> my secret life.
> It's lonely here,
> there's no one left to torture
> Give me absolute control
> over every living soul.
> And lie beside me, baby,
> that's an order. [14]

Realizing that imaginary and symbolic attempts at redemption go nowhere, that they just repeat endlessly, along linear time, the horror of control, I understands that redemption comes in the future as an apocalyptic event which will shatter the repetitive continuum:

Things are going to slide in all directions
Won't be nothing
Nothing you can measure any more
The blizzard of the world
has crossed the threshold
and it has overturned
the order of the soul. [15]

I believes, however, that it is possible for us to prepare for the future moment of redemption. And the way to do this is for masculine desire to attempt an open engagement with the feminine other. I then performs a double action, counting on the services of the death drive. Not only does he enact a death of imaginary masculine desire, but he also enacts a death of the alienated feminine body trapped in the aura of poetic beauty. As the imaginary feminine body loses its aura and becomes commodified, there is the possibility then for the emergence of the feminine other as subject. But in what form will masculine desire return? I again insists on the presence of the veil:

There was a veil between them
composed of good thread
not carelessly woven
Therefore they did not ignore it
or poke at it,
but honored
what hid them,
one from another

Thus they served their love
as those old Spanish masters served
The One Who Does Not Manifest. [16]

In the good thread of the veil, I highlights the pure work of the signifier, which works solely on the basis of an erotics of hiddenness, the not manifest, a nothingness. What emerges for I is neither masculine desire nor feminine other, at least not in their imaginary and symbolic manifestations, but an uncanny relationship to a desexualized feminine, represented by the figure of the angel.

Angelica stood by the sea
Anything I say is too loud for her mood
I will have to come back
a million years later
with the scalp of my old life
hanging from one hand. [17]

I's desire has moved from a fixation on the imaginary phallus —masculine desire wooing the feminine other with its fine words and powerful systems—to the evacuation of masculine desire—nothing to say, stony silence, impotence—and then to the feminine presence of the angel, intuition of the real, who comes to us light as the breeze.

She stands before you naked
you can see it
you can taste it
but she comes to you light as the breeze
You can drink or you can nurse it

it don't matter how you worship
as long as your
down on your knees
So I knelt at the delta
at the alpha and the omega
at the cradle of the river
and the seas
And like a blessing come from heaven
for something like a second
I was healed, and my heart
was at ease. [18]

Wait a moment, though. In experiencing the feminine presence of the angel, is I not fleeing from the horrors of the social-material world, fleeing from the troublesome pleasures of the body? Despite its apparent leaning, this does not seem to be the force of I's reflections. Rather, I is employing a way of thinking and a way of seeing which reveals the truth of the body and the social-material world though its relationship to the paradise of the real. In this way of thinking and seeing, I does not attempt to create a unified understanding oriented to a self-made, authentic masculine identity. Instead of the search for authenticity, I's desire will embrace plural forms of pleasure that are neither masculine nor feminine, as that binary is tied up with an imaginary and symbolic coding. These would be forms of pleasure that escape the work of the imaginary and the symbolic, which in their quest for control and mastery, attempt to hide from the uncanny presence of the angel. Through the death of one form of pleasure, imaginary and symbolic ego pleasure, I discovers other forms of pleasure that are signs of the paradise of the real. The cold theatre of death thus magically and instantaneously slides into a new theatre, a theatre of desire that is pure mask, pure performance. This is a theatre of desire that is not at all removed from the material body and its pleasures, nor the social body and its pleasures, but arises from within the material body and the social body, a material body and a social body that now reveal nothing but masks and performances.

I believes that the way to enact these masks and performances of desire is by participating in the life of the crowd or the masses on the urban street. Here, I exhibits a fascination with masks and performances which does not bring him imaginary or symbolic fulfillment, but instead allows him a moment of enchantment that is, at the same time, a moment of shock and catastrophe. It is an uncanny experience of being away from home but still feeling at home.

Significantly, the life of the street does not give I the contentment sought after by those enamored by the cultured authenticity of the home. Rather than seeking the fullness of meaning in the bound and secure individual who must always in guilt and good conscience retrace his footsteps through hard work and respectability, I seeks to become a mass man of the street, engaging in a process where his footsteps continually disappear, where he can erase his individuality within the crowd, and avoid the trap of disciplined subjectivity. Rather than searching for an interior refuge in the home as an asylum for auratic art and beauty, I, as a man of the crowd, will wipe away any identifying marks that attach to him. I now can take pleasure in the crowd.

In the crowd he is able to develop a new way of seeing, a transformed mode of perception. Within the multitude he demands his rights to the city. This is the living face of the multitude as subject, a creativity of the masses in their resistance to disciplined subjectivity. I, along with other subjects on the street, wishes to claim legitimacy for the variety of masks and performances which escape the normative binary of masculine and feminine.

The tavern is one place on the street where this new way of thinking and seeing displays itself, where the commodification of culture is accentuated to such a degree that the sheer fragmentation of social reality in all its ruin is present. When I and other mass subjects come to the tavern, they bring with them the horror that continually and repetitively governs the social-material world in which they live, and as they drink and dance and converse, they find a way to access the moment of redemption which escapes this horror, the moment when the angel appears.

The tavern is also the place where I experiences the death of feminine beauty and the subsequent presence of the angel. Because it is not the home of auratic art and the retracing of the footsteps of authentic subjectivity, because it displays in such an extreme form the commodification of culture, it announces, in the swirling sensorium of masked and made-up bodies, the death of the poetic ego and the death of imaginary and symbolic solutions.

In the tavern, I will not be able to woo the feminine other with his fine words, or capture her with his beautiful bodily machine, or spell-bind here with stories of his conquests. Here, his desire displays itself as inherently lost, without foundations, without security and fullness, and in this experience of emptiness and nothingness, his desire emerges without pretension, as that which both fills the hole, but yet leaves it empty. It is in the tavern at closing time that I's desire experiences a poetic death. But yet it is also in the tavern at closing time where he is able to meet the angel of compassion who points to a future redemption:

> *So we're drinking and we're dancing*
> *and the band is really happening*
> *and the Johnny Walker wisdom running high*
> *And my very sweet companion*
> *she's the Angel of Compassion*
> *and she's rubbing half the world against her thigh*
> *Every drinker, every dancer*
> *lifts a happy face to thank her*
> *and the fiddler fiddles something so sublime*
> *All the women tear their blouses off*
> *and the men they dance on the polka-dots*
> *and it's partner found and it's partner lost*
> *and it's hell to pay when the fiddler stops*
> *It's closing time.* [19]

And, thus, despite the continuous horror of the past and the present, and the inevitable horror of the future, there was love in the past, there is love now, and there will be love in the future, because of the compassionate presence of the angel.

NOTES

1. Interpretation of this third moment of I has been guided by thinking through the intersection between Lacan and Walter Benjamin. Specifically, see Christine Buci-Glucksmann. *Baroque Reason: The Aesthetics of Modernity*. Trans. Patrick Camiller. Intro. Bryan Turner. Sage Pub. Also on W. Benjamin in relation to the mass and the popular see Jesus Martin-Barbero. *Communication, Culture and Hegemony: From Media to Mediations*. Trans. Elizabeth Fox and Robert A. White. Intro. Philip Schlesinger. Sage Pub., 1993.

2. Leonard Cohen. "Death of a Lady's Man," *Stranger Music*. McClelland and Stewart, 1993, p. 227.

3. Ibid.

4. Ibid.

5. Ibid, p. 228.

6. Ibid.

7. Ibid.

8. "The Rose," *Stranger Music*, p. 262.

9. "There Are No Traitors," *Stranger Music*, p. 165.

10. "One of These Days," *Stranger Music*, p. 180.

11. "End of My Life in Art," *Stranger Music*, p. 284.

12. "Your Death," *Stranger Music*, p. 270.

13. "The Future," *Stranger Music*, p. 370.

14. Ibid.

15. Ibid.

16. "A Veil," *Stranger Music*, p. 189.

17. "Angelica," *Stranger Music*, p. 251.

18. "Light as the Breeze," *Stranger Music*, p. 375.

19. "Closing Time," *Stranger Music*, p. 378.

PART TWO

BRUCE COCKBURN
THREE MOMENTS OF S

The trouble with normal is it always gets worse.

First Moment:

Loving Father

I n the beginning, we find S, our subject, rushing home from the city to the country.[1]

look out the window[2]

The window provides him a mirror-frame in his quest for care and protection, a day dream space filled with images from the other which will reflect back a sense of coherence, meaning, fulfillment in the midst of anxiety.

I'm going to the country[3]

He is leaving behind the dark world of complication and into the world of natural images that soothe.

sunshine smile on me[4]

Into a world where warmth is provided by the sun. Along with the window frame S experiences the containment of the sun which smiles on him, a paternal warmth that comes from the sky. Out of the darkness of the place beyond the country where chaos and incoherence reign, where he cannot find recognition, he fixes his gaze on the sun, the great light that shines down and provides recognition, and there occurs a mirroring that stems the chaos. A relationship is established between earth-mother and sky-father in which the imagery of the maternal earth (which provides nurturance) is released from any excessive hold on S through the influence of the paternal sky. So, while returning to the country, S is ever in motion, with the car window providing the frame.

wind in my hair tells me how it feels [5]

The wind as an elemental force of the sky provides a lightness of being, movement, so that, as he returns to the country hearth with all of its maternal protection from the terrifying world of symbolic complication, he is not bound nor tied but gains a sense of freedom.

birds singing
I'm singing in my bones [6]

Birds of the sky, released, driven to song, and in identification with the birds song reaches deep down into S's bones. Bodily life released to song by birds of the sky.

doesn't much matter now where I'm going [7]

A pleasurable drifting in nature, a sky-oriented paternal movement of the spirit in the midst of the maternal warmth and comfort of the country. The pleasurable drifting in nature is again pursued by S as he embarks on a bicycle trip:

drift along
hear the gravel crackle [8]

S lazily drifts along a country road.

butterflies [9]

Catches a glimpse of butterflies, unique in their released flight, not in any predetermined direction, linear in nature, but an ecstatic dance,

shades of the Eternal Dancer [10]

Wild lines of flight that are at the same time contained by the land and the sunlight:

God has buttered the land with sunlight [11]

In this context,

corn grows high [12]

Toward the sun that releases its energy of growth. The clever parrot is able to sing and knows the words but does not understand the nature of the poetic which is movement, drifting, release:

but he doesn't seem to see
me
making my great escape [13]

In contrast to the sun-king of movement and freedom we have a different kind of king who seems to be given authority in the world beyond the country:

who needs a king
sitting in a tree

so loquaciously
pigeonholing everything [14]

The world beyond the country is one that provides security through firm categories where everything is orderly and fits. But in the country, where we have a unique blend of the maternal and the paternal,

pi-
geons have a way of taking wing
-ingg wing [15]

Back in the safety of the country home, S is again looking out a window, a contained frame that allows him to find security in the other projected back from the images outside:

I'm looking to be by a window [16]

This is a window

that looks out on the sea [17]

The sea is maternal ground to wanderings of S. He does not, however, become submerged in the sea, absorbed by it, but focuses on the sea, on the possibilities provided there for security at the same time as movement.

surf of golden sunlight
breaking over me
man of a thousand faces [18]

The sun as paternal love shines down and reflects off of the maternal sea. As it does so the one light disperses into a thousand rays of love that are

breaking over me [19]

They wash over S sitting by the window. The mirror reflection is one that brings a comforting love that is not binding and fixing, but breaks, in a sense, shatters any ego rigidity, so that, within the scope of containing love, we discover the nurturing of an ecstatic movement of body and self. These rays of light a

> *man of a thousand faces* [20]

Indicating the paternal nature of this sun-light-love, the one sky-father love in its movement through the earth-mother sea becoming multiplied into a thousand fatherly faces that, in breaking over S, actively call for an ecstatic jouissance of movement and freedom. Yet, although there is a revelation of truth through the guiding influence of the sun, S, framed by the gaze of the sky, soon discovers that the sky forces worry about too fast and easy an exposure of truth and wish to turn to the imagery of hiddenness reflected in darkness, storm, thunder and rain.

> *in the Garden paths take form*
> *but the hailstorm guards its own*
> *things forbidden, things unknown*
> *you must travel on alone* [21]

The hailstorm is protective of truth as easy exposure, where idols are constructed that seek to trap and ensnare truth.

> *swelling thunder, truth is hid*
> *behind the glass eye of the idol* [22]

The truth's essential nature is to be hidden and respect given to

> *things forbidden, things unknown* [23]

This insight gathered in gazing out the window at the unfolding of the storm convinces S that

you must travel on alone [24]

Travel not through the safety and security of the group, but by yourself, alone. A movement then in the forces of the sky from sunlight creating forms to a shattering of those forms in the darkness of the storm, which releases the energy bound up in one form to travel on to other creations. This traveling of creative energy taken up not by the group but by the lonely wanderer who moves on to new things still framed by the mirroring of the sky.

Awakening in the country home, S experiences a new morning as the beginning, as what starts things off, as that which is primary and sets the ground for what comes later. And in the morning there is sun and wind with an intimate relationship established between the activity of the sun and the activity of the wind.

the sun is long sailing [25]

The presence of the sun speaks to the presence of love, love as movement forward, not staying in one place, not being stuck or fixed. Sailing is aided by the wind which does not at this point bring on the full force of the storm and remove the love of the sun, but, rather, removes the clouds, which are carried within, that block the love of the sun.

the only clouds you see
are carried within
soon they'll be blown away

wind's gonna rise and blow those clouds away
wind's gonna rise and blow your blues away [26]

The clouds, working in tandem with the wind, are sent by the morning sun-star to enact a journey of love that is a movement through the day to the night. The elemental forces of the storm-clouds and the wind are initiated to move desire forward from day to night, from paternal morning sun to maternal evening moon.

While out canoeing S is able to take in the calming and restoring influence of water and moon:

My canoe lies on the water [27]

Evening approaches where

the sun like gold dust slips away [28]

We approach the night where

one by one the antique stars
herald the arrival of
their pale protectress moon [29]

S understands that the moon is the maternal nocturnal pair to the sun. S is bonding to the other of nature, to the other's face, a mirroring that provides peace, security.

in the place my wonder comes from
there I find you
your face shines in my sky [30]

Yet, this is not a fixed security, without movement:

come with me
we will sail on the wind

we will sway among the yellow grass
when you be beside me
I am real[31]

Rather, we witness a wandering of the spirit that is secured by love. The wind is tied to the sun as shining other who contains. There is a lightness that is produced, a sense of being unburdened in the presence of both sun and wind.

you shine across my time[32]

A temporal continuity of the sun as love and nurturance stays with S, is something he can depend on while in the movement, something that provides security in the midst of absence.

In the sky, birds have a special relationship with the stars, the home of the gods.

high winds
white sky
wild birds do glide[33]

It is here in the movement of wind and clouds and birds that life begins and has its origins. They

move like life beginning[34]

A daughter is born from the union of the morning star and the evening star who becomes the mother of the world:

daughter of the stars
you are
life beginning[35]

S's orientation is toward the sky as the big space of love for wandering:

the sky
is reflected in your eyes
and I
want to fly [36]

The sky is the other to whom S can fly. Held by the other but at the same time provided with a big space to fly, to move and move.

you point to the sea
I see
what seems to be so free
bound by
empty sky [37]

The co-existence of the open sea and the open sky brings freedom—bound yet free.

lord of the starfields
ancient of Days
universe Maker
here's a song in your praise [38]

A strong orientation is displayed by S to the paternal power of the sky, an affirmation of the existence of a creator who stands behind the existence of heaven and earth and has formative power over it.

o love that fires the sun
keep me burning [39]

Important here is an awareness by S of a power that transcends nature, and transcends the sun itself (before the power identified with the sun). This is called love which is the active agent in the sun, and by extension, is the active agent in human desire. It is what keeps us burning for something more than what presently exists. Burning for love, for justice and the overcoming of evil.

S absorbs a feminine that is light and free through its association with the activity of the loving paternal sun:

She is passing in a warm breeze
bars of light that cross the floor [40]

The warm breeze as combination of sun and wind releases the feminine and the maternal. It is both immersion and transcendence, a maternal-paternal intertwining.

by her middle hang the keys
made to open any door [41]

It is from the feminine and the maternal that doors will be opened.

she lives in a house of colour [42]

It is from the base of her house that access to the exciting outside will be achieved.

silence
carries
no apprehension here
in the warm sun by the window sill
I can just sit still
and watch her go by [43]

Sitting there daydreaming, lost in the childlike wandering that is free and unencumbered, warmed by the sun, framed and contained by the window sill, S's gaze is directed toward the feminine other. It is to her that we look for movement in the outside.

> *Queen of field and forest pathway*
> *understands the speech of stones* [44]

Language, as the means for movement in the exciting outside, is her domain.

S asserts that, despite any troubles that may be brought by storms, love as a shining sun will hold him:

> *come on, come on, wind and rain*
> *I know the sun will shine again*
> *till then my lady and my lord will keep me sane* [45]

A connection between the sun and a lady-lord combination. The sun expresses itself through a maternal-paternal intertwining, through a nurturing loving father, a loving third, that is always already there in the identification with the maternal. The transferential relationship is to a love that holds at the same time as frees up for movement. Going down to the shore of the lake,

> *along the breeze came, away my cap went,*
> *my head it was set free* [46]

Anticipations of the future: the sun will shine again, and then a light breeze will clear S's head of burdens, a breeze that is wholly different from the wind of the storm. The combination of sun and wind again allows a secure wandering, a freedom held.

> *my lady and my lord will keep me warm* [47]

Held by the mother-father intertwining, the loving father.

The internalized sunrise provides soothing for S so that the cry of anxiety can be overcome:

we'll walk down the meadow with sunrise inside
so dry your eyes
the winds of all the kingdoms meet where we stand[48]

Sunrise is linked to the force of the winds which will meet at the acute point of internalization so that sun and wind can provide soothing and comfort at the same time as freedom and movement.

Upon a hillside, S experiences the sun as Christ:

up on the hillside you can see the cross shine[49]

Situated up above—rising—providing light and warmth.

you and I, friend, sit waiting for a sign[50]

Looking up above to a transcendent object with which to identify in order to move out into speech, language. S gazes upwards and the identification with the sun-bathed cross initiates a longing for language, for symbolic activity, for speech.

see how the sunset makes the lake look like wine[51]

Through identification with the shining cross as sunset the power of language is unleashed where a movement from lake to wine, water to wine, occurs, a transformation where the material world is raised up to significance through the power of language, which in turn has been initiated by a transferential ideal of the sun. The production of wine indicates a festive raising up, a celebration of this transformation.

over the mountain I can hear myself called [52]

The call of the other, the call of the sun, the call of the loving third, paternal love, moving desire joyfully, festively, out into the material world.

I want to come running but my window's too small [53]

Here there is a sense of being constrained by the existing maternal-paternal envelope created. This was a frame that provided security and nurturance—maternal—as well as a measure of movement and freedom—paternal—but now there is a longing for desire to move outward more vigorously, a desire to embrace the complexities of the outer world of social relations that go beyond nature's embrace.

I must get going, you know, there's not much time
the road is waiting and I'm running out of rhyme [54]

The feeling of constraint is accompanied by a feeling that things must forge ahead now past the initial set of movements outward toward more extended movements. The road is waiting for S and it is the road of language, rhyme, poetic creation. S realizes that human dreaming needs, in terms of identification, to be oriented towards nature's rhythms, a timeless change, both continuity and discontinuity, permanence and movement.

we can't dance without the seasons upon which to stand
Eden is a state of rhythm like the sea
is a timeless change [55]

Moreover,

> *if we can sing with the wind song*
> *chant with thunder*
> *play upon the lightning*
> *melodies of wonder*
> *into wonder life will open* [56]

We realize that we

> *dream ourselves and each other into being* [57]

But yet

> *dreaming is a state of death, can't you see* [58]

unless it identifies with the transcending influence of the sky, the wind, thunder, and lightning. Dreaming then opens up

> *into wonder life will open* [59]

when it finds it's place in the other and the imaginative faculties then are sparked through this outward/upward identification. S is then able to sing, chant and play because he has been lifted up. Poetic language unfolds,

> *melodies of wonder* [60]

And then S experiences a first-moment melancholy, a first-moment encounter with a significant absence and distance, a widening of the circle.

> *one day I walk in flowers*
> *one day I walk on stones*
> *today I walk in hours*
> *one day I shall be home* [61]

Up until now, nature images embodied movement and distance, but there was little in the way of movement within the differentiation of the social that goes beyond nature. Love was provided in a child-like manner in the sense of protection from those complications. The movement into melancholic identification is double: first, a movement toward social material relations, and, second, a movement away from love and toward an encounter with evil and injustice. The structure of love will need to deal with both of these conditions.

Yet, the movement into melancholic identification is situated within the moment of nature, in the context of pre-oedipal identification, and under the influence of the loving father. It is from this vantage-point that S presents a first-order critique of an unjust world, a first-order critique of war and violence:

> *they're losing their pawns in Asia*
> *there's slaughter in every square* [62]

A critique of the deceptive abuses of power:

> *let the world retain in memory*
> *that mighty tongues tell mighty lies* [63]

In this context,

> *it's going down slow* [64]

There are two senses in which things are going down: First, there is evil, injustice, a downfall of love, the removal of love from the world, the absence of the sun, absence of the loving father. But, as well, there is a dawning realization that love must move outward into the complicated world of social relations, of politics and power, of intersubjective conflict, that the circle of love must be widened to encompass all that, which it has not up to this point done with a tighter circle. However, this dawning realization is at this point tempered by suspicion, by a distancing parody of the phallic postures of the boys in power. Having experienced the festive delights of poetic creation there is a sense of how petty and insignificant this activity is from the perspective of redemption:

> *go get the fire department*
> *to bring that hose along*
> *and them and the schoolboy bandits*
> *can water each other's lawn* [65]

Even at this moment, however, S realizes that, although there is a falling into the world of matter, this falling is contained by the warmth of the sun:

> *the bird of paradise spreads his wings wide* [66]

Caught by the bird of paradise, graceful swan, melancholy loon, swift dove, cheerful robin, messenger of paradise, plunging toward earth like the rainbow, announcing the sun after the rain.

> *when the rain shines*
> *the earth sighs gratitude*
> *and spreads her hues bright* [67]

The sun and the bird of paradise always come after the rain, and the rainbow brings the power of the gods to earth, announces their coupling. Experience of the sun-rain rainbow, the bird of paradise, is an identification with paternal love, and as he spreads his wings wide the earth spreads her hues bright.

In the protective embrace of the country, S associates the devil and evil with a splintered sun and a buried sun:

staring at the splintered sun
you could drown yourself in jewels
trying to find the buried sun
you could drown yourself in jewels [68]

Although S now encounters a sun that is damaged or hidden, the implication is that, through his dialogue and through his struggle with the devil, the sun and evil might become unsplintered, with the sun able to shine again. Yet, the illusory path is a search for jewels as ego possessions, where redemption is tied to the bound ego cut off from the other, from the transcendent sky, from identification with the sun in the otherness of the sky. The devil turns our attention toward the pleasures of the earth, jewels taken from the earth—gold, silver—as possessions of our puny isolated ego. Jewels are turned into idols to be worshiped, reflecting happiness of the self cut off from the other, happiness in the commodity, the great pimp of money. Then,

looking down at what you've won [69]

the ego believes it can claim happiness.

and he screams `why don't we celebrate' [70]

Visioning another kind of celebration, where the true sun is found:

standing on a rock in a river
staring at the rain made one

on the surface flashing diamonds
rolling down the twilight canyon
and we shall kiss the sun in spite of him [71]

The house of ecstasy and redemption will be built on a rock, not sand, a rock which provides a secure ground for an orientation to the sky from which comes the light. The light travels down the canyon, down the shoot of time and space, and disperses on the water, creating flashing diamonds. The surface of the water is the meeting point of maternal and paternal, maternal water and paternal sun, producing an ecstasy, a jouissance, that is beyond the ego pleasures of jewel, gold, money, commodity. And the sun has been kissed, in spite of the enticements of the devil. Yet, has this ecstasy been won in spite of the presence of the devil or through the work of the devil, where the work of the devil is part of the journey? Maybe the search for material jewels is a step along the way to discovering the flashing diamonds on the surface of the river. Possibly the material labour involved in searching for the treasure in the earth, believing we have found treasure, but finding out that these were illusory, is necessary labor, with ego disillusionment being a pre-text for post-ego ecstasy?

all the diamonds in this world
that mean anything to me
are conjured up by wind and sunlight
sparkling on the sea [72]

An idea of redemption emerges for S: flashing diamonds produced by paternal sun on maternal water. The contact takes the one ray and creates plural flashes that evoke ecstasy. The wind enters again, for the dispersing rays of sun are carried to various and multiple destinations by the wind spirit.

> *I ran aground in a harbor town*
> *lost the taste for being free*
> *thank God He sent some gull-chased ship to carry me to sea* [73]

S gets stuck on the material earth, in towns where societal relations complicate the spirit. There, it is so easy to get trapped in material relations, in intersubjective relations. Stuck in a home, job, career, marriage, family, friendships. To lose your freedom by entering into concrete relations. Thank God S is sent a ship to carry him out of society and its lures and to the open sea, where material and intersubjective relations are absent. Freedom at this point is achieved by S having access to a set of natural-symbolic relations. In this, the ship is a transitional space, like the window frame, which allows him to safely ride on the surface of the water, to not either be submerged in the maternal sea, nor like the birds, to fly off to the gods.

> *his ship comes shining* [74]

Results in the emergence of a shining ship, a shining self, an emergent self transformed by the paternal light likened to

> *a pearl in a sea of liquid jade*
> *a crystal swan in a sky of sun* [75]

S is able to drift freely on the surface of the water taking in love light and dispersing it out to the world.

S is convinced that he doesn't want the following:

don't want to be on no rooftop
don't want to sit by no fountain
don't want to go to no parties
don't want to be in no `in' crowd
don't want to live in no mansion
don't want to live on no sidewalk [76]

These are all instances where the spirit gets trapped. Instead,

just want to stand where the sea-spray
gleams like fire with you
just want to stand on some hillside
in Wales with you
just want to stand at the rainbow's
real end with you [77]

The sea-spray captures the light of the sun, the hillside allows him access to the sky, and the rainbow is the contact between water-rain and emerging sun. These are moments of redemption in contrast to the traps of social material relations.

small windows, looking outward
show me a sequined sky
rubies shine in my glass of wine [78]

The window frame is a container for S. From the vantage-point of his immersion in material space and time, the window provides a frame for the gaze outward towards revelation. The sequined sky is a golden sky that transports love-light through the window frame and deeper into S, allowing diamond rubies to shine the love light in water, water now turned into a festive, celebratory wine of ecstatic redemption.

music leaps out
in a shimmering intrigue
words unsaid whirl away like dust[79]

The freedom of expression, the freedom of language, is unleashed by the power of light-love-water-wine. Music and words disperse and move about in an ecstatic dance.

you can stumble, you can fall
or you can make the nations crawl
but when death comes in to call
he don't care about it[80]

Does the omnipresence of death mean that all attempts to bring redemption to the material world are doomed, that all are under the sign of death, that all are illusory attempts to find salvation where salvation cannot be found? Or is death a stalking drive that haunts the establishment of ego power, the erection of monuments to success, destroying those foolhardy projects in order to clear the way for love?

oh, Satan take thy cup away
for I'll not drink your wine today
I'll reach for the chalice of light
that stands on Jesus' table[81]

Whereas before no distinction was made by S between different kinds of wine, here there is a clear distinction made between the glass of wine that captures the love light, explicitly linked to Christ, and the illusory wine, linked to Satan. S separates the world of light from the world of darkness, a splitting of good paternal identification with Christ's love and a bad paternal identification with Satan associated with the power in the world. He has an increased awareness of the differing paths that are possible for his masculine desire as it moves out into the world of material and intersubjective relations. Before, his desire was able to have movement and freedom, but within a tight circle of love that, for the most part, avoided material, intersubjective relations, experienced movement and freedom mostly within the context of nature imagery—sun-sea-wind. Now, as his desire moves outward and the circle expands, there is a splitting, with two circles created, one a continuation of paternal love-imaginary father, imaged in Christ, the other a different father, a stern father, who does not give love, but demands compliance, and in return offers a worldly success that is pure ego—obey me and you will get this and that and the other and your happiness will be secured by those possessions—gold, money, commodities, all idols of the spirit.

There is a difference, then, between a Christ-like ideal that is tied to love and a Satan-like superego. Daddy as love versus daddy as ego power. According to this view, death's presence is a death drive that shatters daddy ego power and the self's fixation on that kind of material success, allowing the loving daddy to triumph. This means that S's experience of death is intimately tied to his experience of love. Or, rather, that as the circle of his desire expands to take in the social material world, and as the circle splits to offer him an enticing other circle of ego power, the death drive becomes for him a necessary tool of love, a sword that is needed to cut through the circle of doom associated with ego power in order to continue to free up his desire in the interests of love. Rather than being an escape from material embodiment itself we have a consciousness, from the perspective of being held by the loving father, that the power established in the material world is unjust, evil, not based on love. As S's desire moves outwards in love, there is thus an increased consciousness of the presence of evil and injustice, as lack of love, as ego power.

The question that now emerges for S is to what extent, carrying with him a self held by love, can he transform the here and now of everyday material relations, so that the freedom of sun, sea and wind are expressed in those relations? From the vantage-point of this kind of freedom, the world as it is stands is condemned by love for the continuation of pain and suffering. Death, then, is not an escape from the social material world, to a heavenly beyond, that leaves this material world untouched, but is, rather, a transformative experience for S, where evil and injustice thought to be eternal and fixed are interpreted from the vantage-point of love to be truly transitory, fleeting, the more essential, primordial, originary, and lasting experience being that of love and justice and peace.

S thus faces the possibility of two seemingly rival interpretations in the face of the splitting of the circle: Death can represent for him the transportation of the circle of love to a beyond, a distanced remove, which stands to condemn the social material world for its pain and suffering, redemption occurring when he leaves the circle of doom and moves to the circle of love and waits for a final settling of accounts in the future where the circle of doom will be destroyed and love will triumph. But, death can also represent the destruction of the hold that the circle of doom has on him so that there is a consciousness of the illusory nature of ego power and the inherent always already triumph of love, redemption being an active work in the here and now of death-love to find consciousness of what is ultimately true. Possibly what is expressed is a necessary tension between the two representations of death in relation to love, where both are needed, both a consciousness of the great distance between love and the evil that is dominant in the world, and a consciousness that, despite the seeming power of evil, love is always already triumphant, if only we could recognize it.

> *as longing becomes love*
> *as night turns to day*
> *everything changes*
> *joy will find a way*[82]

S now believes strongly that only death will release him from the pain and the suffering of material life, that only death will ultimately bring joy. Yet, this is death not as escape, but death as a psychic force where pain is wiped away, evil is destroyed, and the warm, soothing light of love is again manifest, and there is joy.

The question at this point for S is how to establish the ground for critique, how to establish a position which challenges the status quo, the way things are, with the overwhelming realization that there can be a better world. In attempting to do this, the question is whether he sets the ideal outside of the present forces from the vantage-point of which present reality is condemned, or whether he sees the ideal working from within the present forces to explode them from within? In terms of death and destruction and its relation to the ideal, must death and destruction come from outside and above to annihilate evil in order for the ideal and love to triumph, or can death and destruction be an immanent force which constantly wreaks havoc on evil and the present forces of injustice? Or, is it possible for S to envision a tension between the two, where the two projects of outside death and inside death are both at work, at the same time, or at different moments, depending on the context, both poles needed for love and the ideal to have life. At this point, the first option seems to hold sway more than the second, outside death rather than inside death, where the ideal, as a circle of love, having been constructed around sun-wind-sea, separates out from the circle of doom and evil and condemns it from afar, from a distance, protecting the ideal from intrusion by the bad. Rather than immanent critique, differentiating from within material social life the progressive good forces from the regressive bad forces, S engages in a mocking parody of the pretensions of ego power, only achievable when he has staked out a removal, an autonomy from all that:

> *look away across the bay, Yankee gunboat come this way*
> *Uncle Sam gonna save the day*
> *come tomorrow we all gonna pay*
> *and it's burn baby burn, when am I going to get my turn* [83]

S presents here his first critique of social-material power, in the form of the United States. But there is little in the way of specifying the actual material forces of evil at work. Instead, he gives us a sweeping critique, under the sign of parody, of any attempt to use aggressive activity to exert influence in the world. The United States might be evil, but in what way is it evil, and how might that evil be distinguished from an assertive, aggressive activity that promotes the ideal, say in the form of resistance struggles and revolutionary plans? The implication is that, from the perspective of a safe and distant home of love, any attempt to exert such an influence, would be foolhardy, and the only solution to the fact that there is evil and injustice is a colossal burning—burn baby burn.

> *something dead under the bed*
> *local diplomats hang their heads*
> *never mind what the government said*
> *they're either lying or they've been misled*
> *and it's burn baby burn*
> *when am going to get my turn* [84]

This tendency by S not to distinguish, on an immanent level, between forces of good and evil, leads here to a mocking dismissal of all political power as inherently corrupt and deceptive. Certainly, political officials have pursued projects of evil that do not promote the agenda of love, but is it possible to conceive of political and government initiatives that do promote the agenda of love, the public good. A distancing parodic attitude does not provide us with any insight into how we might go about this; in fact, it implies that any attempt to do so would be illusory because the ideal, the circle of good, has split off into another, distanced realm, from which, in the end, it can only send down its apocalyptic thunderbolts—burn baby burn.

S envisions a falling dark. Is the falling dark, as a movement into the world of material relations, a necessary journey of the spirit that, despite being rife with anxiety concerning distance, space and absence, carries with it the light of love, so that the light of love couples with the darkness to creatively produce, to creatively objectify in labor? Or is the falling dark, as a movement into the world of material relations, a leaving behind the light of love, a movement from the world of love into a wholly different world where that love no longer exists, where darkness is separated and radically split off from light.

> *and the lights lie tumbled out like gems* [85]

Indicates that S believes that the light of love is moving out into the world, from the one light into many diverse lights, differentiated and plural.

> *earthbound while everything expands*
> *o many grains of sand, slipping from hand to hand* [86]

The light of love is traveling to the earth from its original and primary home in the sky. S has drifted up into the sky and has been allowed a loving paternal freedom there. Now, his spirit moves toward earth, expanding as it descends, the grains of sand metaphorical substitutions for spirit at the same time as metonymic displacements of desire that slip from hand to hand. Thus, S is tied to the light through metaphor: the many both are and are not the one, bonded to but separated, identified with but free form. As well, S is tied to the light through metonymy: the light displaces itself in movement through the many, from one to the other, always moving, always indeterminate, never fixed. Yet this affirmative perspective is challenged by another perspective where the light loses its force as it moves to material expression:

> *catching the light and falling into dark*
> *the world fades like an overheard remark*
> *in the falling dark* [87]

Does this mean that the light has expressed itself, can express itself, through an affirmative material movement, but that within the space and time of that expression, encounters forces of evil where the light begins to fade? What are these forces that cause the light(s) to fade?

all that glory shining around and we're all caught taking a dive[88]

This could represent a suspicion on the part of S that the very dive itself, the very movement of light into darkness, causes the light to fade. Or it could be an awareness that the light is there shining in the material world but there are particular forces within the material world which cause that light to lose its power. The indication is that there is some force within subjectivity itself that leads to the dive. This is expressed in the following:

such a waste!
don't you know that from the first to the last we're all one in the gift of Grace![89]

All humans have the light, the light has expressed love in the many grains of sand, but for some reason, that light is wasted. What has caused that light, which is there and available, to be wasted in human?

working out on Gavin's woodpile
safe within the harmony of kin[90]

S feels safe within the embrace of those friends, lovers and family who know him well, where he feels protected and safe. Protected from what, safe from what?

visions begin to crowd my eyes
like a meteor shower in the autumn skies
and the soil beneath me seems to moan
with a sound like the wind through a hollow bone [91]

Suddenly S is transported from safety to malaise. A transformation of his spirit and at the same time a transformation of that which his spirit identifies with. The whole of nature turns from warm sun, light wind or breeze and open sea to sinister forces: death coming, arriving, speaking of the end. The autumn sky fills up not with the sun as love but with a shower of meteors. Is this the apocalypse? S seems so overwhelmed here with anxiety over the possibility of the loss of love that the vision turns to apocalyptic scenarios of destruction—end-time scenarios. The soil itself moans in the manner of someone about to die.

In fact, death seems present already because the moan is identified with the wind which, rather than producing a lightness of being, courses through bones that are hollow and empty. And yet, although we witness S once again splitting good love and bad world, is there not a sense, in his presentation, that the death scenario, as a haunting vision of apocalypse, rather than being wholly other to the work of love, is a supplement to that work, clearing the way for the light of love to enter the world, wiping away the debris, hollowing out the bone.

In this sense, the meteor shower is the sun itself as anger, the soil moaning because of a wind that is the same light wind of love, but now that wind of love as anger. Sun and wind turn to anger because of the gap between paradise and the state of things on

79

earth, where injustice rules. The anger expressed through remembrance of a "bleak-eyed prisoner" who has been sent away on the basis of having lived a difficult life:

> *you drink and fight and damage someone*
> *and they throw you away for some years of boredom* [92]

Here, there is the recognition by S that the world is bad not because we have individual bad people doing evil, but because there is within the heart of the social, within the heart of our relations with each other, within our intersubjective co-mingling, the absence of love, the absence of the holding and soothing and thus freeing spirit of love:

> *no job waiting so no parole*
> *and over and over they tell you that you're nothing* [93]

S's anger that has become aggressive in the form of meteor showers and wind through hollow bones is then directed at that state of the lack of love. It is like the anger of the Hebrew prophet Amos, who condemned the people for the injustices perpetuated against the poor and those who are outside of power, and who speaks of God's power turning into the power of death and destruction in order to combat this evil. This vision of death is a vision that seeks to clear the way again for the work of love so that sun and wind can find their appropriate expression in people's lives, especially those who have been denied that love.

> *and I toss another log on Gavin's woodpile* [94]

This is angry, aggressive chopping. There is anger in the presence of a privileged government official, *with his mouth full of steak* [95]

indifferently saying to those concerned about the poisoning of the fish in the English River:

if you can't eat the fish, fish in some other lake [96]

This indifference is carried even further by the official who is protected by status and power from the agonies of the people who have been poisoned by eating the fish:

To watch a people die—it is no new thing [97]

The prophet's anger grows:

and the stack of wood grows higher and higher [98]

In this moment, however, there is little to reveal that love comes after death, only a consuming anger at the way in which the ideal is being destroyed:

and everywhere the free space fills
like a punctured diving suit and I'm
paralyzed in the face of it all
cursed with the curse of these modern times [99]

The space that was free and safe before now fills up with evil, like a punctured diving suit.

S is traumatized by the severity of this transformation and ends up in a state of paralysis. There is little sense that love will express itself again in the here and now, such that he or others could actively work to bring about its expression, to see the sun shine again, to feel the cool breeze, to experience the freedom of the open sea. Here, rather than apocalypse and death clearing the way for love in the material world, anger seems to be all there is, an anger that cannot turn itself into action.

a train whistle cuts through the scene like a knife [100]

The cut is needed in the present configuration of things in order to make possible another way. The cut is a whistle of the train, the train of death taking us away, away from all this evil.

and I'm left to conclude there's no human answer here...
but there's a narrow path to a life to come
that explodes into sight with the power of the sun [101]

Through the narrow path opened up by the cut there flows the power of the sun, the power of love. This event is left to the future; there are no human answers to the pervasity of evil and injustice at this point. S will wait passively for an apocalyptic event where the accumulated anger of the world finally explodes to wreak its havoc and then the sun will shine again. At that point there will be a resurrection and death will turn to life.

the earth is bread, the sun is wine
it's a sign of hope that's ours for all time [102]

At that point, the earth that is broken will be restored and the sun which became blood will finally turn to wine at that time.

an elegant song won't hold up long
when the place falls and the parlor's gone [103]

S believes that it's good to labor on creative projects but all these projects are things that make life more pleasant as we wait for the true redemption that comes only when we leave all that we have here and meet again in a completely different place:

we all must leave but it's not the end
we'll meet again at the festival of friends [104]

Where is this completely different place? Is it an escape from the social-material world or is it a place that can only come about through a monumental change in circumstances and relations in relation to which pretty little songs by singer-poets have little effect? Possibly big songs are needed, big songs that speak more forcefully and aggressively about change from evil to good.

smiles and laughter and pleasant times
there's love in the world but it's hard to find [105]

Again, is this love as escape from this world or love as redemption for this world that will take a great deal of work and a monumental change in the state of affairs of the world to achieve?

these days of darkness surely will not last
Jesus was here and he's coming again
to lead us to his festival of friends [106]

Will the darkness not last because the revolution is coming, a revolution that has some material base, or will it not last because we will be able to escape the darkness into a heaven that is always ever beyond this tragedy of life?

With these questions hovering, S has a dream of creation, a dream of creation that speaks of an active love, a movement of love that is not split off from the world, but that is the world:

centered on silence
counting on nothing

I saw you standing on the sea
and everything was
dark except for
sparks the wind struck from your hair
wings around you
angel voices mixed with seabird cries
fields of motion surging outward
questions that contain their own reply.[107]

S's position has shifted here. He is experiencing, within the embrace of the loving father, a movement from passivity to activity, a movement that centers yet surges outward. An identification occurs with a divine subject on the sea, a divine figure who is the center point for the strong elemental forces of sun, sea and wind. A concentration of elemental forces in S and a subsequent strong, active push outwards of those forces to the world. Until now, his movement was outward to the sun-sea-wind. And a loving capture by these forces of the paternal sky allowed safety and security at the same time as a measure of freedom and movement. Yet, the capture of S in the paternal ideal produced a fairly closed circle for S, a movement inwards that was focused on protecting the ideal from contamination by the outside. This resulted in the dominance of passive aims, an activity that tended to be consumed by the need to continually protect and secure an imaginary paradise. The ideal was, then, split off from the social material world for fear of a loss of purity, and activity and movement consisted in a continual splitting, contrasting the pure ideal from the polluted social material outside.

Now, we begin to see on the part of S an aggressive push outwards of the elemental forces of the ideal to the world from the point of concentration of those forces in the subject. Identification thus occurs with a unique kind of subject, an subject oriented toward active aims rather than passive aims, two quite different types of activity. The subject stands tall on the sea, and like Christ, is able to walk on the water without the need of a securing boat, who does not sink into the sea, but is able, on his own, to wander on the crest of the sea. From this position of autonomy, the subject is ready for action. In the darkness of the night there are sparks of love-light that extend out from the subject to the world. The love-light then does not need to be oriented toward the passive aim of holding the self, but is so part of the subjectivity of the self that it is able to aggressively burst outwards giving the subject wings to fly.

> *you were dancing, I saw you dancing*
> *throwing your arms toward the sky*
> *fingers opening, like flares*
> *stars were shooting everywhere*
> *lines of power, bursting outward*
> *along the channels of your song*
> *mercury waves flashed*
> *under your feet*
> *shots of silver in the shell-pink dawn.*[108]

This surging outward of energy turns to into an ecstatic dance, which is, as before, still focused on the sky, but is a dance of the active human subject. It is an active subject that throws his arms toward the sky. It is an active subject that shoots flares of star-light out everywhere to the world, all over, expansive. It is an active subject that bursts into song. The poetic act is thus the expression of a subject who is actively creative in the world.

> *and just beyond the range of normal sight*
> *this glittering joker was dancing in the dragon's jaws* [109]

The active dance of S is a confident dance in relation to evil, not a passive withdrawal.

> *let me be a little light of your breath*
> *moving over the face of the deep*
> *I want to be a particle of your light*
> *flowing over the hills of morning* [110]

S now desires to be the divine breath moving, the divine light flowing, an active subject taking strong hold of the divine power of sun, wind and sea.

> *but everything you see's not the way it seems*
> *tears can sing and joy shed tears*
> *you can take the wisdom of this world*
> *and give it to the ones who think it all ends here* [111]

It is possible to understand this in the mode of splitting—the world ends and then there is the ideal in another place removed from this world. However, given the shift toward active subjectivity it may be more fitting to interpret "ends here" as referring to the status quo, the world that has lost the light, has moved into a state of evil and injustice. And if the light of love is now inextricably bound up with an active subject then the implication is that the world without light can change through the activity of subjects with light, those who actively bring light to a broken world.

ahead where there should be the thickness of night
stars are pinned on a shimmering curtain of light
sky full of rippling cliffs and chasms
that shine like signs on the road to heaven [112]

S witnesses a strong and dramatic display, against the backdrop of night, the light that points to heaven.

I've been cut by the beauty of jagged mountains
and cut by the love that flows like a fountain from God
so I carry these scars so precious and rare, and tonight I feel like
I'm made of air [113]

The light from heaven is a divine light that cuts through the self—a cut of love. This cut scars S, rips through him, but in doing so explodes the heaviness which engulfed his spirit, a heaviness which had led to an overwhelming pessimism about any chance of changing things in this world of evil. The cut is an extension of the influence of the loving father which allows for the widening of the circle, allows for a separation from that tight circle of maternal love that allowed only restricted movement and activity. Yet, this cut is not to be viewed as a severe phallic cut, calling for a severance of ties to what we know as maternal love. The cut of love is one guided by the loving father, a loving third, a love of the mother that now fosters distance.

as we're spit out into the jigsaw flow [114]

We are yet guided by

the shimmering curtain of light. [115]

NOTES

1. This first moment of S has been inspired by a reading of two essays in Julia Kristeva's *Tales of Love*. Trans. Leon S. Roudiez. New York: Columbia Univ. Press, 1987, specifically "Freud and Love: Treatment and Its Discontents" and "God is Love." The end section on S as an active rather than passive subject has been influenced by Teresa Brennan. *The Interpretation of the Flesh: Freud and Femininity*. Routledge, 1992.

2. "Going to the Country," *Bruce Cockburn*.

3. Ibid.

4. Ibid.

5. Ibid.

6. Ibid.

7. Ibid.

8. "The Bicycle Trip," *Bruce Cockburn*.

9. Ibid.

10. Ibid.

11. Ibid.

12. Ibid.

13. Ibid.

14. Ibid.

15. Ibid.

16. "Man of a Thousand Faces," *Bruce Cockburn*.

17. Ibid.

18. Ibid.

19. Ibid.

20. Ibid.

21. Ibid.

22. Ibid.

23. Ibid.

24. Ibid.

25. "Happy Good Morning Blues," *High Winds White Sky*.
26. Ibid.
27. "Let's Go Laughing," *High Winds White Sky*.
28. Ibid.
29. Ibid.
30. "Love Song," *High Winds White Sky*.
31. Ibid.
32. Ibid.
33. "High Winds White Sky," *High Winds White Sky*.
34. Ibid.
35. Ibid.
36. "You Point to the Sky," *High Winds White Sky*.
37. Ibid.
38. "Lord of the Starfields," *In the Falling Dark*.
39. Ibid.
40. "Life's Mistress," *High Winds White Sky*.
41. Ibid.
42. Ibid.
43. Ibid.
44. Ibid.
45. "My Lady and My Lord," *Sunwheel Dance*.
46. bid.
47. Ibid.
48. "The Fall," *Sunwheel Dance*.
49. "Up on the Hillside," *Sunwheel Dance*.
50. Ibid.
51. Ibid.
52. Ibid.
53. Ibid.
54. Ibid.
55. "Life Will Open," *Sunwheel Dance*.

56. Ibid.

57. Ibid.

58. Ibid.

59. Ibid.

60. Ibid.

61. "One Day I Walk," *High Winds White Sky.*

62. "It's Going Down Slow," *Sunwheel Dance.*

63. Ibid.

64. Ibid.

65. Ibid.

66. "When the Sun Falls," *Sunwheel Dance.*

67. Ibid.

68. "Dialogue With the Devil," *Sunwheel Dance.*

69. Ibid.

70. Ibid.

71. Ibid.

72. "All the Diamonds," *Salt, Sun and Time.*

73. Ibid.

74. Ibid.

75. Ibid.

76. "Don't Have to Tell You Why," *Salt, Sun and Time.*

77. Ibid.

78. "Stained Glass," *Salt, Sun and Time.*

79. Ibid.

80. "Lament For the Last Days," *Joy Will Find A Way.*

81. Ibid.

82. "Joy Will Find A Way," *Joy Will Find A Way.*

83. "Burn," *Joy Will Find A Way.*

84. Ibid.

85. "In the Falling Dark," *In the Falling Dark.*

86. Ibid.

87. Ibid.
88. Ibid.
89. Ibid.
90. "Gavin's Woodpile," *In the Falling Dark.*
91. Ibid.
92. Ibid.
93. Ibid.
94. Ibid.
95. Ibid.
96. Ibid.
97. Ibid.
98. Ibid.
99. Ibid.
100. Ibid.
101. Ibid.
102. Ibid.
103. "Festival of Friends," *In the Falling Dark.*
104. Ibid.
105. Ibid.
106. Ibid.
107. "Creation Dream," *Dancing in the Dragon's Jaws.*
108. Ibid.
109. "Hills of Morning," *Dancing in the Dragon's Jaws.*
110. Ibid.
111. Ibid.
112. "Northern Lights," *Dancing in the Dragon's Jaws.*
113. Ibid.
114. Ibid.
115. Ibid.

Second Moment:
Troubled Son

Having passed through the door to the outside with the confidence of an ecstatic vision of eternity, S begins to experience in a dramatic way the darkness of the world and its distance from that vision.[1] Instead of a light traveling that was possible on the one side of the door where he was held tightly in the circle of love, he now experiences grim traveling, a traveling that bears an acute awareness of the contrast between ecstatic eternity and present conditions. The divine light of love is now carried forward confidently by S whose sense of enlightenment is completely wrapped up with that love. He has the eyes of love and is able to view the goings on of the world through those lenses.

> *ministers meet—work on the*
> *movement of goods*

> *also work on the movement of capital*
> *also work on the movement of human beings*
> *as if we were so many cattle* [2]

From this new vantage-point, S sees a movement not of ecstasy and justice, but the movement of goods as commodities, as capital, where humans also get moved, just as if they were cattle.

> *grim travelers in dawn skies*
> *see the beauty—makes you cry inside*
> *makes you angry and you don't know why* [3]

Carrying with him the beauty of the ideal, S sees that others also carry this beauty of the ideal. He has an active recognition, within the otherness of the world, of the beauty of the ideal. He now recognizes that there are other subjects, other grim travelers, other fellow travelers, who carry the ideal, have been nurtured in it, have subjectified it, have carried it beyond the door into the outside. This recognition is significant because it establishes an intersubjectivity based on love, and shows clearly that S has moved beyond the previously established tight circle of love which, although filled with natural correspondences, was still quite lonely, built around the narcissism of one held subject, the day dream world of omnipotent childhood. Rather than just one subject, there are many who carry the ideal into a world which is in need of its expression. This intersubjectivity of the ideal forms the ground for a community of love. Not only, then, does S move from passive aims to active love, activity, in order to be effective for the ideal, needs to be grounded in the intersubjective community of love. Not just one subject in the safe world of natural love, but multiple subjects who form a social bond in order to realize the ideal, in order to bring love to the world. An activist community fighting for change, for a better world.

And because S realizes that the travelers who go together are on a grim journey, he also realizes that their perception of beauty brings with it automatically a perception of the pain that mixes with that beauty. This is what makes S cry, the fact that the ideal of love, intuitively understood as the beauty of paradise, faces conditions of ruin, where that beauty is obscured, and is especially hard to see by those who do not have the eyes of love. This is why he is angry, building up a kind of rage against this condition. In saying that S doesn't know why he's angry, we might get the impression that his anger is quite unfocused at this point, and is not directed at any consciousness of the possibilities of substantive change in social material relations. From this perspective, there is a kind of aimless rage amongst the grim travelers, directed at the perversion of the ideal of love:

> *bitter little girls and boys from the*
> *Red Army Underground*
> *they'd blow away Karl Marx if had the nerve*
> *to come around*[4]

The grim travelers are ones bonded in their consciousness of the ruin, but whose response is an aimless rage, a cathartic expulsion of the pain through a desire for physical destruction. Their recognition of each other as grim travelers is actively directed at a desire to wipe out that which seems to pose as evil.

In a sense, this is understandable and justifiable, for who does not experience the distance or split between love and evil in this world, the distance or split between expressions of community grounded in intersubjective love and recognition, and expressions of community grounded in ego power, where my subjectivity is pitted against yours. And in order for the community of love and recognition to triumph over the community of evil, evil must be wiped out, destroyed.

But how to wipe it out and destroy evil? Is there not the danger, in setting up a community of grim travelers who display rage at injustice and evil, of tightening the circle again, leaving it unable to transform anything except through the false omnipotence of rage hurled from behind the barracks of our pious and self-congratulatory enclaves. Intersubjectivity needs to expand outwards more vigorously and with more determination, in order to encounter more fully, in a more immanent manner, the workings of evil in the material world, but also the presence of love and beauty, which may lie in strange places. Otherwise, intersubjectivity will be based on the traveling of sameness, those who find solace in their like-minded conviction, their similarity of belief. Otherwise, intersubjectivity collapses into ego rigidity, safety in the secure borders of conviction. The active movement out to the world needs a more full and dramatic encounter with difference, otherness, must feel the pain even more sharply and intensely, in order for love to be more than an imaginary ego fantasy.

S is moving toward a position of intersubjective love that fully encounters otherness.

> *smiles mixed with curses*
> *the crowd disperses*
> *about whom no details are known*
> *each one alone yet not alone*

behind the pain/fear
etched on the faces
something is shining
like gold but better
rumors of glory [5]

He recognizes the pain and the fear, yet he also sees the shining light that runs through that pain and fear. The shining light of love is not an external reality which is passively contemplated from the position of safety and security, but is immanent within, is mixed up with his consciousness of a broken humanity. Thus, the shining light of love risks its position of safety and security, its passive contemplation and bliss, and has descended into the depths of brokenness. Smiles come with curses, individuals are alone and yet not alone.

you see the extreme
of what humans can be
in that distance some tension's born
energy surging like the storm [6]

S now has an acute awareness of the distance, of the gap between love and evil, between the ideal and the perversion of the ideal. He sees the extreme expressions of evil at the same time as the extreme expressions of love and they establish themselves as extreme in their tension with each other. Thus, a dialectic is established in which the two extremes of love and evil are not at all unrelated to each other, with the split being a primordial one, unavailable for mediation. There is an energy established through the tension, through the extremes, and it is this energy of the dialectic of love and evil that must be encountered, expressed and worked through. Glory is, at this point, only a rumor, real but not real, there but not there, assured but at the same time not yet possible.

> *you plunge your hand in*
> *and draw it back scorched*[7]

S understands that he needs to make a plunge into the mess, to fully experience all its contradictions, all its ambiguities, all the ways in which love is there then gone, present at the same time as absent.

S's plunge into the mess of material life brings forth an intense sadness which seems to overwhelm him, a loneliness that speaks to a feeling of being abandoned by love but which, at the same time, assumes the very existence and presence of that love. He establishes a more-not more polarity, which is not an unbridgeable dualism, but an opposition in which the not more establishes its presence only in relation to the original presence of more. In this sense, the more came first, is the primary reality, was in existence from the beginning, and the plunge into the not more is a plunge from the original heights of more, an original abundance of love that needs to be re-activated.

> *there must be more…more…*
> *more songs more warmth*
> *more love more life*
> *not more fear not more fame*
> *not more money not more games*[8]

S feels strongly that he need more songs, warmth, love and life in relation to the present experience of fear, fame, money and games. If the original love that seeks to expand and embrace the other is sustained by the loving father then the present condition is dominated by the oedipal father and the legacy of the oedipal father, the superego, which works through fear of the other, and a fixation on control and mastery over the other. A contrast is drawn between a love which leads to songs of life, and the ego which leads to a search for fame and money. Yet, if in one sense the more comes before the not more, and is that which the not more gains meaning in relation to, in another sense, the more comes after the not more, achieves its fulfillment only after the not more has had its day. Here, the more, rather than being pre-ego, is trans-ego, an experience that has passed through the illusory yet enticing work of the ego to arrive at a more self-determined and self-aware understanding of love. In response to the work of the ego, having viewed this from the background of originary love, S can actively work with other recognized subjects on the material expression of love, which allows a more fulfilled presence to love in the world.

> *there must be more…more..*
> *more current more spark*
> *more touch deep in the heart*
> *not more thoughtless cruelty*
> *not more being this lonely* [9]

In this sense, there is no love without despair, without sadness, without loneliness, which spurs S to find love again in the imagination, in song, in projects for change.

S now believes, that in order for love to re-express itself in a new mode, he needs to experience the loneliness and pain of physical embodiment with all its raw emotions, especially hate.

so I find out what the luxury of hate is
as exciting maybe as doing the dishes
face toward window—light received
you walk away to see a film see some
people see a man
stab in throat twist in gut all too clear
not too clear—all been done before
planet breathes exhaustion [10]

In fact, S realizes that the raw emotion of hate needs to be experienced in all its intensity so that the social-material world gains a tangible presence for him. In the omnipotency of his tight circle of love, with his face turned toward the window where the light was received, the social-material world was avoided, warded off from the movements of the spirit. Now, as he moves away from that day-dream window and goes to see a film, a different framing of the world, love encounters evil, which is both necessary absence of the idyllic presence of sun-sea-wind where other subjects were missing, and unnecessary lack of love in what subjects do to each other in the world of intersubjective relations, the stabbing and the twisting of desire.

And it is the experience of this necessary-unnecessary polarity, in its to and fro movement, that provokes hate. It is only as necessary absence that love can expand and create a wider circle for the movement of the spirit. Yet, it is also as unnecessary lack of love that this absence expresses itself. Hate, then, is the experience of a necessary unnecessity, or an unnecessary necessity. Hate is the ambivalent emotion which indicates that love is actively moving forward through the actions of S who can see that, at this moment, lack of love seems to rule, and who thus realizes that only through determined action with other determined subjects that lack of love will turn again to love, a love that is now more fully expressed for being fought for within intersubjective, communal relations. At this point, however, S's journey is experienced as exhausting, as an endless parade of evil that people do to each other.

> *staggers on*
> *enemy anger impotent gun grease*
> *too many thoughts*
> *too dogshit tired*[11]

It seems that S has descended into the depths of depression, and is staggering from event to event, which now all seem meaningless and exhausting, filling him up and weighing him down. In this movement,

> *you get bigger as you go*[12]

You fill up with rage and hate.

> *pain takes shape of grimy window*[13]

The window is now a grimy window full of pain. Does the subject need to fill up with pain and rage until the point of bursting into another mode?

> *disharmony gives way* ·
> *to mute helplessness*[14]

S's desire has moved from a exhausting staggering of grim travelers to a helplessness.

> *what about the bond*

what about the mystical unity
what about the bond
sealed in the loving presence of the Father [15]

The bond referred to takes on the weight of the original development of the bonds of ecstasy signified by the presence of the loving father. The original bond was grounded in a loving father. The difficulty experienced here by S, the helplessness, does not come, as is so often thought, form an original paternal weakness where the subject was fused with the maternal object, and now, in the throes of being cut off from that maternal fusion, experiences extreme anxiety. There was an original relationship with a loving father, a maternal-paternal intertwining, the mother's desire as an expanding space, a primary holding container of love. And it is this original love that experiences a blow, that encounters a second-moment absence. After having taken the blow, though, this original love, as a space and container, actually has the possibility of expanding out into the world of social material relations. A second-moment absence, one that is more pronounced than the first-moment absence which was so securely wrapped by the original space of love, of course means that there comes a more profound and dramatic and troubling experience of loss and pain. Especially as that connects up with, hooks up with, the pain of the world, the suffering, misery and injustice experienced in the world of social material relations.

There is here a stark ambivalence generated by the experience of absence as it encounters these more pronounced conditions: there is both an opportunity for new and exciting experiences of active love in the outside world at the same time as there is a more acute awareness of the presence of evil in that world, expressed in unnecessary suffering, misery and injustice. It is within the heart of this ambivalence that S's desire, as a desire of love, is now situated. And it is precisely an encounter that he needs to deal with through aesthetic creation, through a reinvigorated poetics, through language. Love, which was already there in the beginning, must renew its active forces as an active desire of the subject, and direct its attention toward those outside spaces where absence seems so rife and discover-create love there in the midst of the pain.

As a grim traveler, S moves to alien places, strange places, places of otherness: Pavia, Hokkaido, Paris. As he identifies with new experiences in a world that has expanded globally, a world much larger than the originally safe and secure country abode, he is led to encounter his own strangeness. And as his desire encounters the scenes of this expanded world, he is given new eyes to see, engages in a different kind of perception. Instead of ecstatic, mystical images of nature, his imagination turns to keen and precise images of town and city scenes, ones that are bereft of love.

> sun went down looking like the eye of God
> behind icy mist and stark bare trees
> inside the dim empty cinema two guys in leather
> jackets glance at each other and shiver [16]

In fact, despite the chill that surrounds, S is aware, unlike before, of the presence, however haunting, of other subjects. There is a concentration of perception—which does not drift up into the sky, and does not float out on the sea—on the detail of facial expressions:

I saw an old lady's face once on a Japanese train
half lit, rich and soft luminosity
she was dozing straight upright head bobbing
almost imperceptibly
wheels were playing fast in 9/8 time
her husband's friendly face
suddenly folded up in a sneeze
across the straight
a volcano flew a white smoke flag of surrender [17]

No perfect angels that only lovingly protect and contain; the richness and softness of the feminine presence is bound up with a disturbing movement of the head which bobs around as if inhabited by some other more haunting presence.

I wonder if I'll end up like Bernie in his dream
a displaced person in some foreign border town
waiting for a train part hope part myth while the
situation changes hands [18]

S experiences a displacement, a metonymic traveling of desire within a world that is now really big. Finds himself in a border town, waiting for a train to somewhere else. Which seems to indicate a borderline state, a state of anxiety that comes form a loss of the original maternal-paternal hold. At the moment of this loss, there is a great danger of moving from an experience of the loving father, to the oedipal father, the harsh father of cold systems who demands compliance:

or wearing this leather jacket shivering with a
friend while the eye of God blazes at us like the sun [19]

THREE MOMENTS OF LOVE

This is not a soothing, warming sun, but a menacing, piercing sun, where an original identification with a loving father has turned into a submissive tie to a hostile father. But are the two experiences really that divided? Possibly, the father experienced as piercing sun is a necessary transition in the state of love, where love as original bond becomes a transformed bond that has moved out into the world of intersubjective relations, a kind of initiation rite, like the initiation rites of old, where the young subject needed to be torn kicking and screaming from the safe and secure abode of original love and experience, trembling before the absence, in order to take up an active position as a social subject.

The jostling of desire in the midst of a transition in subject position can by quite dramatic. Take the otherness of Tokyo:

> noise and smoke and concrete going on forever
> grinding gears and drivers getting high on exhaust [20]

S has an awareness here that is so different from that gained from idyllic nature, where, alone in his dreams, he had a sense of expanded space, desire moving out to the cosmos. In Tokyo, everything is so busy, so crowded. There is such little space between people that it is hard to feel the freedom of the spirit.

> oh Tokyo—I never can sleep in your arms
> mind keeps on racing like a fire alarm
> me and all these other dice bouncing around in the cup [21]

There is no rest for the weary spirit. Instead, S faces a bad dream of anxiety where his mind races from distressing scene to distressing scene, with the overwhelming feeling, not of security and containment, but of being bounced around, jostled to and fro.

fascist architecture of my own design
too long been keeping my love confined
you tore me out of myself alive [22]

From the new vantage-point of second-moment absence, S views his earlier self as fascist.

This is quite a harsh criticism, one that seems, at first glance, severe and unwarranted. Yet, the charge of fascism can be viewed as determined by the mood and perspective of a subject in crisis, a subject in process, a subject becoming other. The charge arises from an intense feeling that his love was, in the past, too confined. A love that was beautiful and ecstatic, but bound in such a way as to be unable to meet the other, unable to love the other, unable to feel the pain of the other, the other who beckons the subject to actively intervene in the world in the interests of love. From this perspective, in its intensity of feeling, that original love is charged with fascism.

From the outside, this seems harsh, for the original experience of love, as a maternal-paternal intertwining, was an original movement towards otherness, yet a limited one in terms of its encounter with other subjects and the world of social material relations. But it is important to catch hold of the critical insight here, because original love, no matter how open, certainly has the potential of moving in a fascist direction. A love that is confined to home, hearth, kin and local community is one that can easily be fearful of the other, fearful of the plurality and diversity outside its confines. And in that mode of perception, love can turn over into evil, through a warding off of the other, the stranger, and a vilification of all those outside forces that threaten the safe world that contains desire. If that were the case, S would love only those who were close, those who were like him, those who were familiar, and see as dangerous, fit only to be destroyed, those who were outside of those parameters.

It is possible, then, to view this original experience of love as the construction of the imaginary ego, a specular construction bound to an otherness that was not expansive and open, but bound to the security of its original identifications. And in that way, what is needed is a cut, a tearing out of S, while still alive, from the secure bonds that tie him to the imaginary ego, to be thrown helter-skelter into the outside world of difference.

Although this understanding is appealing, we need to situate the present anxiety of S as a moment for him when there is a disillusionment with the earlier bonds in terms of the possibility that those bonds might become fascist. This may be an understandable disillusionment, but it obscures the extent to which the fascist direction is only a possible development of those earlier bonds, and not a necessary development of them. Certainly, when we look say at many evangelical right wing interpretations of the gospel of love, we find the fascist mode of development highlighted. But that is not the true legacy for the gospel of love, which, there from the beginning, is fatefully destined to move out into otherness, identifying with otherness, and especially the pain and distress of the other. Is not the early expansive love of sun, wind and sea, a love which desires to move out expansively into the world of intersubjective relations in a transformative way? And does not this new active movement of desire still feel fundamentally held by love, where embracing the other is an embrace that does not move outside the circle of love, but expands the circle to include the other, to include otherness itself? And we can see here that S, although experiencing extreme anxiety and distress over the loss of ideals, still, in the last instance, feels held by love and is still ok:

> *I've been in trouble but I'm ok*
> *I been through the wringer but I'm ok*
> *walls are falling and I'm ok*
> *under the mercy and I'm ok* [23]

And as,

> *the magnificent facades crumble and fall* [24]

there is, through it all, an experience of

> *the billion facets of brilliant love*
> *the billion facets of freedom turning in the light* [25]

Emerging for S is a clear-eyed, wide-awake perception of the concrete material encounters in love relationships.

> *woman cry—chase man down street crying `no Chuckie, no, please don't'*
> *another girl comes they run along St. Andrew, turn south on Kensington*
> *meanwhile Chuckie beats it down the alley by the chicken packer's* [26]

S is now in the heart of the city, in all those spots that are seemingly outside of grace. The street has been tagged a place of pollution, a place of corruption, where people are led astray by the lures of erotically enticing entertainment in pubs, taverns, clubs. Not only that, the city street is where the crowded apartments of the workers are, those who do not have the means to buy their way into bourgeois comfort, bourgeois interiorized spaciousness. If progress equals a process of interiorization linked to the private family home and street, then the crowded street in the heart of the city is outside of progress, outside of the fulfillment of subjectivity. And if the fulfillment of love and romance between individual subjects is eclipsed by the history of romantic love defined by the bourgeois, defined by the rituals of courtship and marriage that sanction off a reified space from the supposedly corrupting influences of the outside, then the love and romance of the crowded city street is again outside of fulfillment. Yet, it is in the midst of those crowded city streets, in the tiny apartments in buildings lined with alleys and interspersed with small shops and restaurants, that we find S searching for answers. And he discovers that, in this world, relationships display themselves openly as difficult and precarious. You invest yourself in a love bond, and so often Chuckie flees, and you're left chasing after that permanence without success.

> *you pay your money and you take your chance*
> *when you're dealing with love and romance* [27]

In his confused state S latches on to amusements:

> *in the maze of moebius streets we're trying to amuse ourselves to death* [28]

The sky is here not, as before, an ecstatic beauty, but a heavy presence, squatting over us:

> *under the deep sky that's squatting closes over us tonight*

you'd think it was trying to hatch us [29]

What it does hatch, what it does give birth to, is numbness and confusion, not a birth into ecstasy and beauty, but a birth that leaves the subject battered and bruised:

the numb and confused, the battered and bruised [30]

But yet if we think of romantic love as an imaginary illusion, as a trap of the spirit, as a ruse of power bent on binding love to a structure that limits and confines, then the fact that S has had a profound experience of the severing or cutting of that bond, the fact that he is left alone now on a dirty, crowded city street where the exalted bond of romantic love is absent, where love and romance are spun out into the world, jostled about by the constraint of difficult material circumstances, then maybe we are left with the realization that S's experience of love is taking a necessary plunge into the elsewhere of matter and has to find its place there. It's not a pretty world—it's a world of casual relationships, of numb and confused friends, of conversations in the night that turn quickly to pulsing rhythms of desire:

confused and solo in the spawning ground I watch the confusion
of friends all numb
moving like stray dogs
to the anthem of night-long conversations, of pulsing rhythms [31]

The desire that S displays here is one that is indecisive, ambivalent, one that brings pain. Yet it is a desire that displays an open willingness, one that subjects itself to the world of otherness, experiences it directly, passionately, without question:

and through it all, somehow, this willingness that asks no questions[32]

In the protected world of the tight circle of love, the strong one was a maternal-paternal presence that held S in his ecstasy and freedom. Now, S has descended into the pain of the world and he is looking for a source of strength, a source of active energy. He is looking for one who, despite the pain, despite all the misery and injustice of the world, is able to love, is able to give. This calls not for a maternal-paternal presence, but a friend-lover on the same plane as the subject, a mutual subject who in turn can be held.

isn't it hard
to be the one who has to give advice
isn't it hard
to be the strong one[33]

S poses his questions from the position of embodiment, where it is hard to believe that a person who loves does not do so without difficulty, hard to believe that love can be given without struggle. Thus the divine maternal-paternal presence needs to become a friend-lover who is like the subject. The coming-into-being of S as a subject of love means that love is taken in as part of the journey of embodiment where struggle and pain and tears and anguish are all part of that being. To be strong, then, cannot but be hard and difficult. Yet, although S is fully aware of how difficult it is for another subject like him to provide that love, he is not left adrift in desire, but finds a friend-lover who provides:

> *when I was a torn jacket hanging on the barbed wire*
> *you cut me free*
> *and sewed me up and here I am* [34]

And what seems even more significant is that S realizes that the other subject like him who provides love, needs to experience an active love in return. Previously, the love of the other was experienced as full, as complete, as sufficient, in relation to which S could depend, as a child depends on its mother and father. Now, S realizes that love comes from friends and lovers who are not sufficient unto themselves, are not full and complete, but need his active presence in order to be able to provide love back:

> *you help your sisters, you help your old lovers, you help me but*
> *who do you cry to* [35]

Emerging for S, then, is an intersubjective structure of love that calls on love to be actively initiated by subjects in a community of recognition and giving.

> *blue billboard on the roof next door*
> *makes a square of light on the kitchen floor* [36]

City lights, very unlike the pure light of nature, come from a billboard, one selling a commodity. S's immersion in the displacing work of material signifiers is here represented as commodities on the market.

Is commodification of the light the necessary objectification of natural forces for the purpose of social exchange, intersubjective exchange? Or is commodification of the light the perverse alienation of natural forces, where spirit does not find expression and recognition in the networks of social exchange, intersubjective exchange? Once again, S sits on the fence, sits precariously between these options which are so very hard to distinguish. On the one hand,

a thousand question marks over my head[37]

S is unsure of his place in this world of social material relations. On the other hand,

all's quiet on the inner city front
I don't know why I should but I feel content[38]

S is content, despite the lack of surety, and despite the anxiety. What is the basis of this ambivalence? It seems to indicate that S, even though he experiences a most profound and dramatic absence and distance—absence of answers, distance from the original maternal-paternal container—still experiences love in the form of contentment. This experience of contentment is a new or transformed experience of the loving father for the subject. The original loving father was one that wrapped the subject in love, leaving some distance and freedom of movement, but for the most part tightly containing. This is an original experience of a metaphorical relationship, a primary awareness of the tensive `is/is not' of love, where love is protection and containment, but is not at the very same time, giving room for freedom of movement However, once S has plunged into the swirl of social material relations, the inherent metaphorical character of the loving father, as a substitution for the love of the mother, changes from one of first-moment ecstasy to one of second-moment contentment, which does not preclude the experience of ecstasy, but forces ecstasy into a more dramatic encounter with absence. This means that the tensive is/is not structure of love has shifted so that relationship of the is of protection and containment to the is not of absence and distance is stretched, with absence and distance becoming more intense, calling out for a new and different response on the part of protection and containment. This new and different response is that of contentment, which distinct from first-moment ecstasy, allows S a sense of peace, a sense of being okay in the midst of a world that does not seem to be okay.

> *midnight flight*
> *fullmoon light*
> *laughter in the air*
> *it's a party all right*
> *slate-blue clouds*
> *iridescent sea*
> *I'm heading for you*
> *and you're heading for me*
> *and we dance and we dance*
> *and we dance....* [39]

S is able to establish and catch hold of moments when he can leave aside the pain, the suffering, the misery, and laugh, party, dance. In the face of a form of intersubjectivity and social interaction that is damaging to the human spirit, S searches for the existence, within this mess, of a form of intersubjective contact, a way for himself as a subject to meet another subject, where each is able to give to the other the opportunity to be released from the burdens of the damaging world, and through the dance, meet each other and recognize each other, so that there is affirmed a realization that love and freedom can be other than what is. This mutual recognition and affirmation is concentrated in the image of the dance. The dance here is a second-moment ecstasy, distinct from the first-moment ecstasy of sun, wind and sea. First-moment ecstasy originated through the experience of the solitary subject who was allowed to experience love shielded from the tensions of the social material world. Second-moment ecstasy comes through intersubjective recognition, a dance not of the solitary subject, but of two subjects together, recognizing and affirming each other as good despite the pervasiveness of the bad, recognizing and affirming love in the midst of all the evil.

Where, then, does injustice come from? From what source does the misery and the pain arise? It is clear, from the position S has arrived at to this point, that evil does not come from an inherently evil world, from which we need to escape. Nor does S believe that evil comes from inherently evil individuals, condemned to do evil by a natural state of sinfulness. Rather, the emerging belief of S is that evil, in the form of injustice, comes precisely from the outward pursuit of justice, especially the pursuit of justice that is guided by the ideal.

> *what's been done in the name of Jesus*
> *what's been done in the name of Islam*
> *what's been done in the name of man*
> *what's been done in the name of liberation*
> *and in the name of civilization*
> *and in the name of race*

and in the name of peace!
everybody
loves to see
justice done
on somebody else [40]

It seems, then, that injustice comes from the attempt to overcome injustice. Justice is lost when justice is pursued.

What's going on here? S has entered a new, bigger world of love through a holding on to, and an extension of, an inherent paradox of being that was already established in the first moment. The paradox is that love emerges when protection and containment exist at the very same time as movement and freedom. Even in the first moment when protection and containment formed a tight circle, and there was an absence of intersubjective recognition, there was a significant awareness of, and possibility for, the ecstatic wandering of the spirit in creative freedom and openness. With the plunge into the complicated social material world, that paradox extends itself out into intersubjective recognition, where love is only possible when S is able to recognize the plight of fellow subjects, and is, in turn, recognized in his plight. This means that the paradox shifts ground from the mode of protection-freedom to the mode of social justice-freedom. That is, S recognizes that the creative freedom of the spirit is only possible when there is a ground established collectively for that freedom to be possible, not only for one subject in isolation from others, but for subjects in relation to each other, that one subject's freedom is inextricably bound up with another subject's freedom.

This relates directly to another paradox that has been central to S's concerns: the tension between the necessary plunge into absence marked by anxiety and pain and the unnecessary plunge into evil marked by anxiety and pain. Love occurs when the one paradox is rubbed up against the other paradox to initiate an active love of reconciliation and redemption. That is, the paradox of intersubjective freedom needs to be situated within the paradox of fighting injustice. A love that expresses itself communally through mutual recognition is always a love that is actively oriented toward releasing the spirit from the unnecessary pain of unjust social material relations.

S understands that the two projects need to be kept in tension with each other for love to occur. Problems occur when the paradox of intersubjectivity is abstracted from the paradox of overcoming injustice and when the paradox of overcoming injustice is abstracted from the paradox of intersubjectivity. Both are occurring here. S's cry of: "what's been done in the name of …" is double-edged: it means both the affirmation that a community has come together to affirm their bonds together intersubjectively and the affirmation that, as a community, they have attempted, from the vantage-point of the ideals of that community, to fight what they perceive to be the evil of this world.

Thus, a double abstraction has occurred which centers around problems in the expression of intersubjectivity. For example, a community of Christians may come together in bonds of love, to nurture and recognize each other. Yet, a problem occurs when that community seals off the project of intersubjectivity and denies recognition to other subjects perceived to be outside the ideal of Christ. The identification with "the name of Jesus" thus moves from intersubjective love to an superego force which demands not love but compliance to a set of abstract standards, and deems those not following the authoritative dictates of a superego father to be unworthy of recognition. The very movement that extends paternal love beyond the one subject to the many thus turns over into a movement which establishes a fortress ego, bound and sealed around a austere, demanding father who denies any extension of love to the outside. In this scenario, any encounter with absence which might embrace diversity is anxiety-ridden, projected out on to scape-goats in the world: gays, feminists, communists, Jews, etc. This brings forward the second abstraction: the fight against evil and injustice is divorced from the project of an extended intersubjective love and becomes a project to rid the world of projected scape-goats. We can observe, then, a set of dialectical reversals which are tied together by the lack of recognition for the other: love turns to hatred of the other, and justice turns into injustice for the other.

> *can you tell me how much bleeding*
> *it takes to fill the world with meaning*
> *and how much, how much death*
> *it takes to give a slogan breath*
> *and how much, how much flame*
> *gives light to a name*
> *for the hollow darkness*
> *in which nations dress*
> *everybody*
> *loves to see*
> *justice done*
> *on somebody else* [41]

Given the pain and misery that has been actively pursued in the name of love and justice S is disheartened by the realization of how the plunge of love into social material relations has gone awry. And he believes that it is important, in the face of all this, to affirm a truer path for the plunge of love, a path that allows the paradox of love to unfold in a much different way. The paradox at this point unfolds with the insight that

charity begins at home [42]

Love and justice can only be established in the context of our direct relations with other subjects, in the community of love that we establish there. Yet, this community does not harden itself against the outside, does not then barricade itself against the other, but from within the heart of those direct relations, creates an expansive openness for love:

got to search of the silence of the soul's wild places
for a voice that can create the spaces
these definitions that we love create—
these names for heaven, hero, tribe and state [43]

S is affirming here that he, along with others, should not avoid the project of creating just, loving communities, but that he and others must create big spaces for that project, where our active work of naming what is the ideal community needs to return again and again to silence and the wild, where things are again left open to difference, not crowded by the same. It is interesting that this means that, as he plunges into the active work of love and justice in the social material world, S recognizes that there is a need to return to that first-moment experience of openness and freedom that came with the original circle of love. In returning to sun, wind and sea S is able to catch hold of the experience of beginning anew, and is open and accepting, like the child, of and to the other.

Even though S believes that justice is not an ego project where walls and boundaries are created in defense against the other, he does still maintain that justice has a normative status toward which we should work, guided by the ideal of love. In the beginning was love which is an originary characteristic of creation. In the beginning was the loving father as a maternal-paternal intertwining, which creates a space that is both protecting-containing and conducive to activity and movement. The loving father also creates a time framework where the space of love can be expanded over time on the basis of human activity. The momentum of love is then for an expansion of the space of love over time to continually embrace otherness and strangeness. This emphasis on human activity in relation to the expansion of love comes through gifts which humans are created with. These gifts exist as potentials for the activity of love. For each human these gifts of love are there in the beginning, but are expressed over time in relation to a space that expands to greet the other. Yet, precisely because these gifts of love are ones dependent for their expression on humans actively expressing them in space and time, there also exists the possibility that those gifts express themselves in a way that does not fulfill the project of love, but the project of evil.

> *way out on the rim of the galaxy*
> *the gifts of the Lord lie torn*
> *into whose charge these gifts were given*

have made it a curse for so many to be born
this is my trouble—
these were my fathers
so how am I supposed to feel?
way out on the rim of the broken wheel[44]

The wheel of love as a cosmic force can be broken through a redirection of the paternal influence. Gifts are handed down so that, through the influence of the loving father, S, along with other subjects in a community of love, can expand the wheel. Yet this paternal legacy has been misinterpreted by superego fathers. Superego fathers forget the maternal ground of love and seek only to expand the wheel through the fixed ego projects of mastery and control over the other, especially the feminine other. Difference and progress are pursued by a clinging to systems, which at every point attempt to move forward only by abjecting what is perceived to be the threatening other. The project of embracing the other through love is turned into a project of expelling and vilifying the other, violently projecting the other outside the circle of love, denying the other his/her status as a subject worthy of love, worthy of recognition, worthy of being included in the expansion of the wheel. This cursed project of our fathers which has wasted the gifts of love is what produces the pain, misery and evil in this world. How to respond?

water of life is going to flow again
changed from the blood of heroes and knaves
the word mercy's going to have a new meaning
when we are judged by the children of slaves

no adult of sound mind
can be an innocent bystander
trial comes before truth's revealed
out here on the rim of the broken wheel [45]

The presence of evil, in the form of the project of superego fathers, means that the challenge for S, in seeking to regain the presence of love through the project of a loving father, is for love to battle evil. The activity that will be required of him to expand the wheel of love is an activity that must meet the challenge of evil. Paradise, as the not yet that impels S to active love, is one that needs to turn the blood of pain and misery into the water of life. This activity that seeks love involves S placing himself outside the circle of evil associated with the paternal superego project. It involves him entering heart and soul and body into all the spaces abjected by the superego father, identifying fully with all those forms of subjectivity that have been placed in the dustbins of historical progress, rendered unfit. Mercy and reconciliation and redemption will have a new meaning now because the whole project of establishing paradise will be viewed from the perspective of the children of slaves. It is not possible for anyone who wishes to pursue love to be an innocent bystander in this struggle. S thus realizes that he must endure the trial of brokenness in order for truth to be revealed.

In order for S to expand the circle of love he needs to identify with the brokenness of the world, view things from the perspective of the outsider, the stranger, the loner.

I'm a loner
with a loner's point of view

I'm a loner
and I'm in love with you [46]

The lonely see things that the comfortable insider cannot. This insight by S is in keeping with the Hebraic prophetic tradition: redemption can only be voiced by those outside of the projects of ego power. From the stand-point of this prophetic perspective, S realizes that he needs to experience, in a most profound and dramatic way, the reality of abandonment and loneliness in order for love to again express itself. Experiencing loneliness is not simply a mystical encounter with nothingness, where ego illusions are overcome through private meditative actions. It is a loneliness that comes through identification with those who have been abjected by the social material reality of ego power. Paradoxically, then, S can again encounter love when he travels to those spaces and toward those subjects who are experiencing the most pain, misery and destitution in the social material world. It is in meeting not the inside subject but the outside subject that S can once again pursue love. This gives a distinctive ground for intersubjective recognition. Recognition of subjectivity as a subjectivity that expands the circle of love can only come through the recognition of the slave. Not the slave as some abstract idealist category, but the slave as that embodied subject who has experienced the most difficulty in this world, who has been left outside. It is in meeting and identifying and working with outside subjects that love will again be possible.

There is a difference between opposing oppression and injustice through denial and opposing oppression and injustice through negation. Negation involves transforming the sense or feeling of injustice into concrete, differentiated symbols or images. From the perspective of identification with the loner and the outsider, S is able to name particular injustices that are directly material in nature. He is able now to engage in an explicit naming of evil:

> *strikes across the frontier and strikes for higher wages*
> *planet lurches to the right as ideologies engage*
> *suddenly it's repression, moratorium on rights*
> *what did they think the politics of panic would invite*
> *callous men in business costume speak computerese*
> *play pinball with the 3rd world trying to keep it on its knees*
> *their single crop starvation plans put sugar in you tea*
> *and the local 3rd world's kept on reservations you don't see* [47]

S's naming of evil takes the form of negation: paradise is not these things. At the same time, there is a prohibition on naming exactly what justice is, in terms of some fixed conception.

In line with the Hebraic prophetic tradition this would be idolatry. God and justice cannot be named, they are always more than what we might conceive them to be. In fact, what gets us into trouble is those projects of justice which bind and border the good into the normal:

> *but the trouble with normal is it always gets worse* [48]

According to S, what gets us into trouble is when we try and normalize justice into a project of the ego-nation seeking order, an ego-nation where

> *security comes first* [49]

When this occurs there is a passing over into injustice and oppression because we become blind to the way in which our quest for order and security violates the other:

> `it'll all go back to normal if we put our nation first'
> but the trouble with normal is it always gets worse [50]

However, the work of justice as an angry work of negation does not mean that this activity of negation becomes the whole story, leaving S with a relationship to Nothingness as the ground of being. If we are to follow the Hebraic prophetic tradition, God is not Nothingness, but a Big Love that establishes itself through a personal covenant. The personal covenant between the divine and S provides the ground for the loner (the subject who negates the normal) to enter into an intersubjective relationship with the other, the stranger, those who fall outside the normal. Thus, justice is characterized not by a fixed project of moral standards that demand acquiescence and compliance, but an attitude towards otherness, a loving embrace of otherness. And it is through this attitude and this embrace of otherness that S is then able to turn to the projects of justice deemed normal in this world and say with conviction and with anger: this is not justice, this is not paradise.

S now believes that a just social world only comes through active subjects critiquing injustice and through it all establishing, wherever they can, intersubjective relations of love. And he is also now convinced that a just social world does not come through a passive relationship to a set of ideals that seek to make us comfortable. The question S addresses here is: doesn't the quest for the ideal society, for paradise on earth, revolve around creating an infantile passivity where everything material is provided for us, just as we demand it?

> *sun climbs toward high noon*
> *glints metallic off the bowl of the spoon* [51]

The sun of love is shining yet there is a demand to be spoon-fed. Yet, S recognizes that the bowl is empty:

> *I hate to tell you but the candy man's gone* [52]

Still, many persist in holding on to a

> *sweet fantasia of the safe home* [53]

A passive absorption of a perfect harmony. You can

> *catch it in a dream, catch it in a song*
> *seek it on the street, you find the candy man's gone* [54]

S seems to be telling us that such a quest for paradise is a misconstrual of the search for the divine and the active presence of the divine in social material life:

> *misplaced your faith and the candy man's gone* [55]

S's experience of Tokyo

> *Tokyo jetlag evening walking*
> *out of my throat appears this chuckle*
> *a true 20th Century sound*
> *a little crazed and having no tonal center* [56]

one of fragmentation, being jumbled, struggling, sliding, with no loving space to contain it, to hold it, to give it some frame.

> *the echoes of this laugh fade for a time*
> *snaking among those jumbled pedestrians*

following that struggling Cedric taxicab
sliding over the seeming infinity of white light and neon [57]

Then he flashes to a fantasy of a prairie Indian hoop dancer:

with no warning, mind's eye winks like a lifespan
and opens again on memory flash of prairie Indian
dancers—they're on a stage, all jiggling motion
and flare of bright feathers, surrounded by white faces
floating on a sea of mind
hoop dancer struts in front—drum and voices blend with endless
rain [58]

The present moment of fragmented sliding from one image to another brings forth in S's fantasy a correspondence with an ancient traditional ritual of fragmented sliding, a jiggling motion of drums and voices and limbs flailing. This opportunity to situate one moment within an ancient traditional moment comes because of a special kind of cut which wipes away the distancing of linear time and homogenous space and connects one being-in-the-world with a primordial being-in-the-world:

there's a time line
something like vertical, like perpendicular
cutting through figures shuffling on horizontal plane
cutting through the survival pride of the dancers
through the guilty, sentimental warmth of the crowd
through to some essence common to us, to original man
to perhaps descendants numberless...or few [59]

Notice the distinctiveness of this cut in comparison to the classical oedipal cut. The classical oedipal cut would sever S from his origins telling him that the original, the primary, was not conducive to progress, development, individuation, subjective reflection, reason. The oedipal cut tells him to situate himself within the complexity and diversity of contemporary existence by employing the ego-superego mix: control and master the complexity and the diversity by always relying on the voice of guilty compliance. The distinctive cut emerging here in S's experience is one where he immerses himself in the contemporary, urban experience of fragmentation, of being jumbled, of struggling, of sliding, and then is immediately transferred to an originary moment where those same experiences are replayed in ancient time centered on the hoop dancer. The present experience thus finds its meaning through a cut to the past, through an originary moment that forms the essence of S's being. However, the originary essence finds its own fulfillment in the fragmentation of the present. It is important that S immerses in the present fragmentation of an urban simulacrum. This is different from a bypassing, or avoidance of, the contemporary moment and a passive flight to the past. It is an experience of a now-time where revelation cuts through time and space to reveal itself from within the heart of the contemporary moment. And the image of the hoop is significant in this cut, in this production of the now-time. For the contemporary experience of fragmentation that is, in the absence of the cut, not held by love, comes to be held by love, through being actively transferred, through fantasy, to the circling embrace of the hoop dancer.

where it intersects the space at hand
this shaman with the hoops stands
aligned like living magnetic needle between deep past and
looming future
butterfly pierced on each drum beat, wing beat, static spark
storm front, energy circle delineated by leaping limbs [60]

An ecstatic wild abandon creates an energy circle, one that holds S and allows him the conviction that the wildness is good, the abandon is good, the energy produced is good, because they do not spin out of the circle of his subjectivity and the owning activity of his subjectivity, but are inextricably bound up with his subjectivity and its active presence in the world. The active movement of S in contact with the divine is a circular one, figured also in the turn of the earth, the hatching of the egg and the circling of the eagle:

he's the earth he's the egg he's the eagle always circling
always turning—always comes back to the center [61]

S has experienced a cut whereby there is a return to the primary which is not an exit out of the present but an infusion of originary love into the present malaise. This is a cut of love and is distinguished from that other cut associated with the stern oedipal father. The cut of love is one that resumes the creative work of original, first-moment love within the differentiation of present social conditions and within the differentiation of present language. The cut of love is thus a poetic act that makes use of images and symbols that speak about the present from the perspective of past paradise and the future paradise of love. This poetic act is an act that originates from the outside to upset the systemic work of ego power in the present, to smash through the idols of worship in the present that blind us to the past of love and the future of love.

In this vein, S implores us to listen carefully for the revealing work of the poetic, for it will most likely come from positions outside of established power:

> *maybe the poet is gay*
> *maybe the poet is drugged*
> *maybe he's a woman* [62]

These are positions from which S is able to engage in a critique of the reigning symbolic system:

> *but you need him to show you new ways to see* [63]

It is important to emphasize that the prophetic voice of the poet is outside the established system. It is only from outside the normal that S has access to a set of images of paradise which can then rub up against the normal and establish a position that is simultaneously poetic and critical.

> *don't let the system fool you*
> *all it wants to do is rule you*
> *pay attention to the poet*
> *you need him and you know it* [64]

S believes that he needs to be vigilant to make sure that he is not fooled by the illusory dreams of paradise offered by the system which are not based on love, but on the troubling normal, on the rule of the ego. The system rules through the ego where subjects are taken in by seductive images of paradise which only, in the end, serve to bind them to a restricted position which is cut off from intersubjective recognition of the other. These ego images are false images and it is only by opening up to the prophetic voice of the poet that S believes he will be able to have access to true images of paradise based on originary love.

S participates in an activation of the sun dance as a dance of love where a troubled masculine desire meets a renewing feminine other. This occurs in a decidedly unromantic setting:

> *dance music from the corner bar*
> *over dogs barking at a passing car* [65]

On a hot muggy night, after a day of hard labor, S's masculine desire finds release from its burdens in a spirit of celebration:

> *hot night—streets are full of life*
> *carnival faces in Rembrandt light* [66]

S's masculine desire finds release from its troubles by becoming-woman, through an encounter with the feminine moon which causes a transference to a different world:

> *half moon shining through the blind*
> *paints a vision of a different kind* [67]

Then unfolds a carnivalesque release of becoming-woman through dance where bodies entangle and the sweat produced by that entanglement reflects the light of the moon:

> *wet limbs striped with silver light*
> *locked together at the center of the night* [68]

This is an ecstatic encounter with S's masculine desire making contact with feminine night to bring about a paradise of gold:

> *and your hair tumbles down like Sahara gold* [69]

A new sun is activated here through contact with the night and the moon. In a sense, this is a reactivation of an ancient sun dance, yet one that is fully embodied, fully immersed within the troubles of the material present. Sun-gold, then, comes from the feminine night, from the woman in ecstatic dance. The type of sun activated by the day-time ego brings about trouble, a burdened spirit in need of redemption and transformation. The day-time sun needs to be transcended by the sun of night, through contact with the light of the moon on the tumbling hair of a woman in dance. A Sahara gold, as the desert, wipes the slate clean for new activity that is based on the paradise of love.

> *step outside—take a look at the stars*
> *catch a glimpse of the way things are—*
> *making contact.* [70]

Making contact with the stars is a paternal contact for S.

> *making contact*
> *swimming in an ocean of love* [71]

Making contact with the ocean of love is also a maternal contact for S Thus, there is the paternal and the maternal coming together here.

> *I hear the drumming of the surf and I have to dance*
> *stepping to the rhythm of circumstance—*
> *making contact* [72]

The maternal-paternal influence leads S to an active movement of dance which does not avoid the present material reality but attempts to have the expansive love which contains and frames him address present circumstances. In fact, with the paternal guidance of the stars in the sky and the maternal protection of the ocean of love, S seeks to actively transform present circumstances in the direction of love.

I feel so good I want to swallow it all[73]

S believes that the world at present is in a state of sleep and desperately needs to awake from the night of sleep, desperately needs the light to shine again and provide renewal, redemption.

rising like light spill from this sleeping town
like the light in a lover's eyes
rising from the hearts of the sleepers all around
all those dreamers trying to light the sky [74]

The light of redemption already exists in the night of sleep, but in the form of a dream consciousness. These are the dreams of the oppressed for a better world. S can feel the power of these dreams:

burning—all night long
burning—at the gates of dawn
singing—near and far
singing—to raise the morning star [75]

As the world passes through its night of sleep it is the activity of the dreamers that will allow the morning to arrive again, to have the sun of love again appear on the horizon. These dreams are poetic intimations of paradise. Their very poetic force makes them powerful. They burn as lights in the night keeping alive the hope for a better world. They turn to song and it is the coming together of all the dreamers singing that will raise up the morning star, the sun of love.

rising like lightning in the pregnant air
it's electric—I can feel its might
I can feel it crackling in my nails and hair—
makes me feel like I'm dancing on feet of light [76]

The songs of the oppressed in the night speaks a language that, with electric lightning-like force, causes love to appear again. Not just for some chosen group, but for all—an all-inclusive love.

singing for the yellow and the brown and the black
for the red and the white people, too [77]

In this night of oppression, S comes to the conclusion that dramatic acts are needed, possibly a revolution. Like in Nicaragua, when the people dreamed a better fate and rose up against an evil regime.

in the flash of this moment
you're the best of what we are—don't let them stop you now
Nicaragua [78]

In order for the morning star to be raised again there must be burning, a burning away of the old which occurs through the forceful activity of subjects who seek to restore the ground of love.

In extreme moments, moments where evil is most present and love most absent, violence may be necessary. S admits that, at moments, his response to the horror of evil and extreme injustice is to court the dream of violence which, in lightning-like fashion, could wipe away the scourge of trouble.

I don't believe in guarded borders and I don't believe in hate

I don't believe in generals and their stinking torture states
and when I talk to the survivors of things too sickening to relate
if I had a rocket launcher…I would retaliate [79]

Yet, S understands that the heart of the revolution does not lie in heroic violence, but in the activity of the common people caught up in the everyday, each doing their part.

battered buses jammed to the roofs
dust and diesel the prevailing themes
farmer sleeping on the truck in front
feet trailing over like he's trolling for dreams
smiling girl directing traffic flow
.45 strapped over cotton pink dress
marimba-brown and graceful limbs
give me a moment of loneliness' [80]

These are all part of the local material responses of people living under duress and seeking to restore love.

dust and diesel
rise like incense from the road—
smoke of offering
for the revolution morning [81]

In this, dust and diesel are transformed into incense. They become ritually purified as an offering for the revolution.

padded with power here they come
international loan sharks backed by the guns
of market hungry military profiteers
whose word is a swamp and whose brow is smeared
with the blood of the poor [82]

Again, S takes on the prophetic voice. Just as Amos condemned the powerful and rich in Israel for the sins committed against the people. The reason for the emergence of this ancient prophetic voice is that the powerful have rejected the law. What is the law? The law is expressed negatively, by way of critique. The law is tied to the idea of justice. And justice is established through a critique of what it is not, of injustice. In the case of the Israelites, Amos tells us that "they sell the righteous for silver, and the needy for a pair of shoes—they that trample the head of the poor into the dust of the earth , and turn aside the way of the afflicted."[83] According to S, the same is true today of big money capital, in the form of the International Monetary Fund:

> *IMF dirty MF*
> *takes away everything it can get*
> *always making certain that there's one thing left*
> *keep them on the hook with insupportable debt*[84]

The prophetic position on justice establishes itself, then, through an understanding of oppression.

Injustice is the oppression of the poor and the needy, those at the bottom of society. Justice, is always a response to injustice. And the response to oppression is one of restoration. Restoration involves destroying the mighty, bringing the high low. Amos reminds the Israelites that God "destroyed the Amorites before them, whose height was like the height of the cedars, and who was as strong as the oaks."[85] The reason that the rich and the powerful must be brought down is because justice is not established through abstract law but through a personal relationship of a people with divine power, through what is called a covenant. The covenantal relationship between God and his people clearly specifies that the people will worship a God who, as S has learned, is personalized as a paternal-maternal parental love, but who is always ever more than what we might conceive him/her to be. The effect of this covenant is that the people will not set up idols to worship, because that would divert them from their reverence for this mysterious love of God. Thus, essential to the conception of justice is a critique of idolatry. This means that the relationship with the divine, with God, is effected by working for justice by fighting idolatry. The wealth and luxury of the rich and advantaged is viewed as a form of idolatry, a worship of their own comfort at the expense of others. Amos has a damning critique of the luxurious life of the rich: "Woe to those who lie upon beds of ivory, and stretch themselves upon their couches, and eat lamb from the flock, and calves from the midst of the stall; who sing songs to the sound of the harp, and like David invent for themselves instruments of music; who drink wine in bowls and anoint themselves with the finest oils, but are not grieved over the ruin of Joseph!"[86] Likewise, S has this to say about the elite in the third world:

> *see the paid-off local bottom feeders*
> *passing themselves off as leaders*
> *kiss the ladies shake hands with the fellows*
> *and it's open for business like a cheap bordello* [87]

In line with the voice of Amos, S understands that the rich and the powerful commit idolatry because they understand happiness as personal happiness. Worship of a covenantal divine or a convenantal God means that our understanding of self is not tied to individual riches and happiness. When the rich and the elite amass wealth at the expense of the rest of the community, they are severely narrowing their understanding of self. They have not opened themselves to an understanding of happiness that exists outside their individual ego selves. In this sense, the ego as a bound, enclosed entity has become an idol which is worshiped narcissistically. Being bound to a covenantal relationship means moving beyond the narcissism of the ego and the understanding of happiness tied up with ego fulfillment, and an opening up of oneself to a care and concern for the well-being of other living beings outside your own ego. The covenant is a great big love, where the energy of love moves outward to embrace the other. The establishment of the covenant and the critique of idolatry are thus joined to a critique of oppression. And the overcoming of oppression is the overcoming of idolatry and the narcissism of ego happiness. This means that it is only as the rich and the powerful are brought down that the process of restoration can occur. The rich and the powerful need to understand that redemption only comes through the happiness of all members of the community. Amos taking on the voice of the covenantal God says: "I hate your feasts, and I take no delight in your solemn assemblies, I will not accept them, and the peace offerings of your fatted beast I will not look upon. Take away from me the noise of your songs; to the melody of your harps I will not listen. But let justice roll like waters, and righteousness like an overflowing stream."[88] So too, according to S, in this present time of injustice and idolatry, the revolution may be needed:

137

see the loaded eyes of the children too
trying to make the best of it the way kids do
one day you're going to rise from your habitual feast
to find yourself staring down the throat of the beast
they call the revolution [89]

At this moment in his journey, S turns to the night for renewal. Renewal comes from the darkness and the light of the moon.

over the slow slide of continents
over the salt pans pipelines masts and pavilions
shimmering crescent moon recedes into working dawn [90]

At this moment, it is the day-time sun that block access to the power and influence or renewal which comes from the light of the moon on the lily flower at midnight.

in the rising day, you keep fading away
don't I know that you're always around
I can reach you if I try
lily of the midnight sky [91]

An Indian myth[92] tells of how one of the stars fell in love with the people and desired to be close to the people, and so slipped away from heaven at night, hovering over the water for a time, finally to settle on the surface of the water as a delicate, white star-shaped flower. The lily is a flower of renewal and redemption that we can access at night by the light of the crescent moon on a glistening lake. It is when the approaching day comes, when all the troubles of the day-time world of injustice and oppression dawn upon S, that he loses sight of this renewal and this redemption.

I raise a fist to the marauding sun that has hidden you away[93]

At the same time, though, as dawn approaches he longs to carry over the renewing power of the delicate lily and the light of the moon and the glistening water into the day-time troubles in order to heal all the troubles.

I'm the rag in a bottle of gasoline
longing to ignite
ich will alles
all of you—shining on the panther skin of night
mirrored in a black lake in a night that glistens like blood on
gold[94]

The power of the lily-moon-water works in the transitional space of night to renew S, to give him strength to enter into the day to fight for justice, to struggle to overcome the troubles brought about through oppressive forces unleashed in the day.

stand on a bridge before the cavern of night
darkness alive with possibility
nose to this wind full of twinkling lights
trying to catch the scent of what's coming to be (in this...)
world of wonders[95]

Again, the night becomes a transitional space of renewal for S. The night serves as a bridge, crossing to paradise, to a world full of wonders.

there's a rainbow shining in a bead of spittle
falling diamonds in rattling rain
light flexed on moving muscle
I stand here dazzled with my heart in flames[96]

It is in the rain at night that otherness is revealed to S, things not evident to him in the troubles of his day-time world. The rain turns to falling diamonds revealing a light that so transforms him that his heart is ignited and burns with aliveness, ready to re-enter the day with the power and energy of love. For the transitional space of the night is a space of love:

> *sky full of love pulled over my head* [97]

Yet, there is an opposite power at work in the night, opposite to the power of the lily-moon-water: an evil occurring in

> *the still dark hours*
> *Sunday in a shanty town* [98]

It is the bullies who come at night, the military thugs:

> *tension builds as the only sound*
> *is the quiet clash of metal and boots*
> *and now and then an order barked*
> *at the bullies in the drab green suits*
> *military thugs with their dogs and clubs*
> *spreading through the*
> *hunting whoever still has a voice*
> *sure that everyone will run* [99]

As reported by S, evil comes at night with the oppressive force of the bully, using terror, violence, confinement and torture to squelch any resistance to their power. And because of this night-horror, dawn comes as a transitional time and a transitional space moving toward release from oppression and entry into paradise, a transitional space-time in which there is resistance to the oppression.

> *at the crack of dawn the first door goes down*
> *snapped off a makeshift frame*
> *in a matter of minutes the first rock flies*
> *barricades burst into flame* [100]

And then, after the battle with the forces of evil in the dawn, the day emerges as a time and a space for the disarray of the night to be overcome and peace and justice to assert their presence again.

> *first mass rings through smoke and gas*
> *day flowers out of the night*
> *creatures of the dark in disarray*
> *fall before the morning light* [101]

The renewing activity of flowering is not here associated with the lily of the night but with the coming together of the oppressed people in a community of faith bound not by the evil of the military state but by divine love. The transition from an oppressive night to a resistant dawn to a reconciling day is marked by the ringing of the church bells which calls the people home to love and away from the dreadful evil of the ten year military regime.

> *bells of rage—bells of hope*
> *as the 10 year night wears down*
> *sisters and brothers are coming home*
> *to see the Santiago dawn* [102]

S presents us with a dream of a Santiago sunrise, a vision of redemption and paradise for the oppressed.

> *I got a dream and I'm not alone*

141

darkness dead and gone
all the people marching home
kissing the rush of dawn[103]

NOTES

1. The interpretation of this second moment of S is inspired by reading Jessica Benjamin. "The Shadow of the Other Subject: Intersubjectivity and Feminist Theory," *Constellations*. Vol 1, No. 2, 1994, pp. 231-254, as well as the essays by J. Benjamin in *Like Subjects, Love Objects*. Yale Univ. Press, 1995. The reading of this second moment was also influenced by Julia Kristeva's *Black Sun: Depression and Melancholia*. Trans. Leon s. Roudiez. Columbia Univ. Press, 1989, especially, "Psychoanalysis—a Counter-depressant" and "Life and Death of Speech."
2. "Grim Travelers," *Humans*.
3. Ibid.
4. Ibid.
5. "Rumours of Glory," *Humans*.
6. Ibid.
7. Ibid.
8. "More Not More," *Humans*.
9. Ibid.
10. "You Get Bigger As You Go," *Humans*.
11. Ibid.
12. Ibid.
13. Ibid.
14. "What About the Bond," *Humans*.
15. Ibid.
16. "How I Spent My Fall Vacation," *Humans*.
17. Ibid.
18. Ibid.

19. Ibid.
20. "Tokyo," *Humans*.
21. Ibid.
22. "Fascist Architecture," *Humans*.
23. Ibid.
24. Ibid.
25. Ibid.
26. "You Pay Your Money and You Take Your Chance," *Inner City Front*.
27. Ibid.
28. Ibid.
29. Ibid.
30. Ibid.
31. Ibid.
32. Ibid.
33. "The Strong One," *Inner City Front*.
34. Ibid.
35. Ibid.
36. "All's Quiet on the Inner City Front," *Inner City Front*.
37. Ibid.
38. Ibid.
39. "And We Dance," *Inner City Front*.
40. "Justice," *Inner City Front*.
41. Ibid.
42. Ibid.
43. Ibid.
44. "Broken Wheel," *Inner City Front*.
45. Ibid.
46. "Loner," *Inner City Front*.
47. "The Trouble With Normal," *The Trouble With Normal*.
48. Ibid.

49. Ibid.

50. Ibid.

51. "Candy Man's Gone," *The Trouble With Normal.*

52. Ibid.

53. Ibid.

54. Ibid.

55. Ibid.

56. "Hoop Dancer," *The Trouble With Normal.*

57. Ibid.

58. Ibid.

59. Ibid.

60. Ibid.

61. Ibid.

62. "Maybe the Poet," *Stealing Fire.*

63. Ibid.

64. bid.

65. "Sahara Gold," *Stealing Fire.*

66. Ibid.

67. Ibid.

68. Ibid.

69. Ibid.

70. "Making Contact," *Stealing Fire.*

71. Ibid.

72. Ibid.

73. Ibid.

74. "To Raise The Morning Star," *Stealing Fire.*

75. Ibid.

76. Ibid.

77. Ibid.

78. "Nicaragua," *Stealing Fire.*

79. "If I Had a Rocket Launcher," *Stealing Fire.*

80. "Dust and Diesel," *Stealing Fire.*

81. Ibid.

82. "Call It Democracy," *World of Wonders.*

83. Amos 2:6,7, *Holy Bible.* Revised Standard Version. World Pub. Co., 1962.

84. "Call It Democracy," *World of Wonders.*

85. Amos 2:9, *Holy Bible.*

86. Amos 6:4-7.

87. "Call It Democracy," *World of Wonders.*

88. Amos 9:13-15, *Holy Bible.*

89. "Call It Democracy," *World of Wonders.*

90. "Lily of the Midnight Sky," *World of Wonders.*

91. Ibid.

92. "The Lily," *When the Morning Stars Sang Together.* Agincourt, Ontario: Book Society of Canada, pp. 118-120.

93. "Lily of the Midnight Sky," *World of Wonders.*

94. Ibid.

95. "World of Wonders," *World of Wonders.*

96. Ibid.

97. Ibid.

98. "Santiago Dawn," *World of Wonders.*

99. Ibid.

100. Ibid.

101. Ibid.

102. Ibid.

103. Ibid.

Third Moment:

Big Circumstance

S has moved from a maternal-paternal comfort to an encounter with absence and abandonment where there is a re-weaving of love that names injustices and works for new love structures.[1] He now moves into a new moment, where there emerges a heightened realization that he doesn't know paradise, that he can't catch it within normal human understanding, that any attempt to do so would be a continuation of the project of idolatry that was associated with injustice in the first place. This is an encounter with the divine real that subverts and thwarts all attempts within symbolic language and activity to nail down the truth of paradise.

> *the man who twirled with rose in teeth*
> *has his tongue tied up in thorns*
> *his once-expanded sense of time and space all shot and torn*[2]

THIRD MOMENT: BIG CIRCUMSTANCE

The man who thinks that he has it all figured out is suddenly brought low. S understands that any sense that he had of being able to capture paradise—know it, own it, capture it in an image, a story, a poem, a song—is shot down, blown to bits by Big Circumstance.

> *big circumstance comes looming*
> *like a darkly roaring train—*
> *rushes like a sucking wound, across a winter plain*
> *recognizing neither polished shine*
> *nor spot nor stain—*
> *and wherever you are on the compass rose you'll never be again*[3]

The character of love has definitely changed for S: from the very beginning, the early tight circle of containment was gradually expanded encountering more and more absence, needing more and more of the engaged activity of S to transform that which was not or no longer love into love again. This meant that S needed to employ language, especially the poetic, to name the evil in the world and to begin to name the alternative of justice where love would again prevail. Now, love for him takes the mode of the death drive which works against language in its constructive phase becoming a deconstructive force that, like a darkly roaring train destroys everything he was so proud of and so attached to. Or, love as death drive is a sucking wound, which, indifferent to the tried and true categories of human understanding, gathers in all that is despised and rejected, all that is abjected by his active human will in its attempt at a clean, orderly and proper paradise, all that is shadow to the stabilizing light, and deposits it at the stable door.

left like a shadow on the step
where the body was before—
shipwrecked at the stable door [4]

These sentiments could easily be construed as a pessimism about the ability of humans to create a paradise of love in material earthly life. But, S is not claiming that we should now give up the fight against injustice, oppression, evil. Rather, the conclusion he arrives at is that the paradise of love is always bigger than what he might imagine it to be, bigger than anything he could possibly create. It will always be better than that and in being better than that keeps us ever vigilant and active in the struggle for love, knowing that what we have is not all that can be.

big circumstance has brought me here—
wish it would send me home
never was clear where home is
but it's nothing you can own [5]

Ownership is idolatry in the sense that it binds paradise to an ego image of what love can be when love is always bigger and better. Yet if ownership—of property, words, images, whatever—will not allow him access to the contours of paradise, S is sure of one thing: that paradise is designed for the outsider and on the ground of the outside. He realizes that if he is going to look for intimations of paradise, he is going to need to look in those places outside of power and privilege, and to those who have been denied influence and significance.

blessed are the poor in spirit—

blessed are the meek
for theirs shall be the kingdom
that the power mongers seek [6]

Intimations of paradise come when S is able to fully identify, psychically and materially, with being shipwrecked, losing all, having nothing, and from that (un)ground, being open to the love of a community of other outsiders and other outcasts from power.

The position S arrives at of being shipwrecked is a decidedly different form of faith then that which has forgone the ethic of an expansive and inclusive love in order to fixate on the righteous path, a self that is closed off to the other.

you read the bible in your special ways
you're fond of quoting certain things it says—
mouth full of righteousness and wrath from above
but when do we hear about forgiveness and love? [7]

The criticism here is directed by S toward any gospel, any message of transformation and renewal, that believes it has the right and true answers to the questions of life. The danger that S recognizes for himself is that he might identify with a particular project of redemption that has very distinct characteristics and forget that the truth always transcends, is always ever more than, the particular project in the here and now he might identify with. Attachment to an active and working symbolic language sets up a training in purity, where those who are attached are able to identify who are in the know and part of the chosen group by their allegiance to the symbolic attributes associated with the redeemed life. S understands that if he became part of such a faith he would then become

inbred for purity and spoiling for a fight [8]

His desire, rather than being oriented toward the outside, the other, would then be turned back on those who agree with him, share his vision, possess his sense of the world. The possibilities for an expanded love of the other would be cut off, and his love would be bound up with those who are like him. His work, and the activity that marks him as a subject of the symbolic, would be oriented toward creating walls and borders around his desire.

shutters on store fronts and shutters in the mind [9]

This all so that desire cannot possibly leak out and be contaminated by the other.

we're so afraid of disorder we make it into a god [10]

If this scenario unfolds, then God will stay silent:

> *sometimes you hear the Spirit whispering to you*
> *but if God stays silent, what else can you do*
> *except listen to the silence? If you ever did you'd surely see*
> *that God wont be reduced to an ideology*
> *such as the gospel of bondage* [11]

Because of the danger associated with the gospel of bondage, S is convinced that we need a more fundamental orientation to the silence, the gap, the absence, the hole. Which comes about through a dis-identification with the gospel as a gospel of exclusive righteousness and a new identification with a position of Nothingness. There he will find God.

S acknowledges that he has spent so much activity trying to do the right thing, constructing systems that would allow him to figure things out, painting pictures of the good paradise. He now knows that the ego gospel balloon that he had so painstakingly blown up with his ideas for righting the wrongs of the world needs to be let go of. Instead of the ego balloon, he understands that he needs to attach himself to the balloon that is filled with darkness, float away from all the symbolic idols on the ground, and finally burst open toward the ecstatic experience of otherness.

> *too many pictures*
> *swirling*
> *momentum of civilization*
> *threw me too far over this time-simple landscape*
> *and I hang here, in this mountain light*
> *a balloon blown full of darkness—*
> *got to let this ballast go*
> *got to float upward*
> *till I burst* [12]

S is left then with the realization that, despite all the thinking he has done in the service of transformation and renewal, he ends up with nothing, ends up understanding nothing.

> *all these years of thinking*
> *ended up like this*
> *in front of all this beauty*
> *understanding nothing* [13]

What is S then to do then with the presence of evil in this material world, the horrible actions, not of the death drive as a psychic force for the realization of nothingness, but the death squad which tortures and kills in defiance of the death drive, clinging to the gospel of bondage.

> *they cut down people like they cut down trees—*
> *chop off its head do it will stay on its knees—*[14]

He and others have tried and tried to respond to the evil in the system:

> *I've go friends trying to batter the system down*
> *fighting the past till the future comes round*[15]

However, in his attempt to fight the evil system, S realizes that things cannot be perfect, that in fact perfection is precisely the quest of the system itself, which brings people to their knees because they do not live up to its demands. Yet, this realization of the illusory quest for perfection according to symbolic fixation, does not mean now that he will shy away from acting in defiance of the evil system.

> *it'll never be a perfect world till God declares it that way*
> *but that don't mean there's nothing we can do or say*
> *down where the death squad lives*[16]

Where there is evil S can bring love, and it is his ability to assert the presence of love in the midst of the evil brought about by all the gospels of bondage, all the systems trying to trample living, loving people, that speaks to the reality of redemption in the material world.

> *like some kind of never-ending Easter passion*
> *from every agony a hero's fashioned*

> *around every evil there gathers love—*
> *bombs aren't the only things that fall from above*
> *down where the death squad lives* [17]

This means that, although his project is unlike the gospel of bondage which creates a violent ego project out of naming paradise, S still recognizes the need to dream paradise. Yet, this is a dream where S identifies with otherness which places a prohibition on creating borders and walls for paradise:

> *this world can be better than it is today*
> *you can say I'm a dreamer but that's okay*
> *without the could-be and the might-have-been*
> *all you've got left is your fragile skin*
> *and that ain't worth much down where the death squad lives* [18]

S dreams images that are inherently self-destructing. He has a vision of a world that is so different from the world of evil and oppression that now rules, but, at the same time, is a vision that cannot be translated into concrete structures. For if dreams became concrete structures then the problem would immediately arise of the borders, the walls, the reification of those structures, those structures lording over the human spirit. S is left, then, with the dream of paradise as metaphor: a tensive is/is not where there is a vision of love which informs his practice here and now without him being able to say that he has it all sown up. The dream as metaphor then serves a negative-critical function: it allows S to condemn the lack of paradise and the lack of love in the structures that are now in place and it allows him to envision a renewing spirit of love and healing for the brokenness caused by those structures. Yet, the dream does not allow him, in fact prohibits him, from going ahead and working toward constructing a new regime which would start the story of the gospel of bondage all over again.

> *used to have a town but the factory moved away*
> *down to Mexico where they work for hardly any pay*
> *used to have a country but they sold it down the river*
> *like a repossessed farm auctioned off to the highest bidder* [19]

It's good to have stable material structures that provide. Stable communities that have a public infrastructure that provide, for the subjects of those communities, irrespective of income, services which increase their quality of life. Stable work places with secure jobs that pay decent wages so that working subjects can provide for themselves and their dependents without the stress of unemployment, underemployment, lack of affordable housing, etc. S is convinced that these are the basic material structures of love that are essential. Any critique of the restrictions and limitations of structure in relation to ego power are not directed to the establishment of love structures that provide a secure material ground for the creative exploration of subjects. And this forms a critical perspective from which to understand change:

> *mighty trucks of midnight moving on*
> *moving on*
> *moving on* [20]

Relentless movement and change, figured in the constant and ever-present movement of transport trucks on highways and freeways, is here viewed by S negatively, as that which robs people of the essential ground of communities and jobs. However, as we have seen, there is a problem associated with the creation of stable structures, when those structures are constructed according to the demands and the dictates of the ego, which is bent on security against the threats of the outside, control and mastery of the other. Thus, stable material structures can become idol-types, symbolic projects that provide an illusory claim to paradise.

> *wave a flag, wave a bible, wave your sex or your business degree*
> *whatever you want—but don't wave that thing at me*
> *the tide of love can leave your prizes scattered*
> *but when you get to the bottom it's the only thing that matters*[21]

Waving the flag of nationalism indicates an ego tie to an ethnic purity that excludes the other, the outsider, in fact views the other and the outsider as a threat to that purity. Waving a bible indicates a fixation on the righteous moral character, so often centered on a fear of sexual diversity, where concerns of social justice and inequality are left unanswered in the overriding quest for the bound and bordered good family, which self-righteously views other types of family and other types of sexuality as pollution and corruption. All these fixations harbor in them the possibility of blinding S to an openness to the outside, to the other, and more particularly, to a concern for those who are denied material comforts and denied their rights. These structures are oriented around fear of the outside and the other and so they end up with an excessive concern with building up walls that are impenetrable. In this context, the presence of the mighty trucks of midnight that relentlessly move on allows for necessary change, represents the presence of a destabilizing force ready to shatter and destroy these ego structures. And this is when

the tide of love can leave your prizes scattered [22]

The tide of love is a force of the big outside, the big other, which, like the death drive, convinces S that any attachment that he might have to structures of national and ethnic purity, sexual and moral purity, are misleading and misguided in terms of true human happiness. The tide of love leaves all these ego prizes scattered to the winds of change.

> *I believe it's a sin to try and make things last forever*
> *everything that exists in time runs out of time some day*
> *got to let go of the things that keep you tethered*
> *take your place with grace and then be on your way* [23]

Taking his place with grace is bound up with the tide of love for S, in the sense that he believes he needs to continually open himself up to the influence of the outside and the other. This means that he should be able to let go of all those attachments that are oriented in an inward direction, to preserving himself and those like him, those who share his attributes. This points to the fundamental difference between ego structure and love structure. Love structure is one that opens S up to the outside and thus allows him to move out into the world with a care and concern for the well-being of all living things that exist, and not just his own kind, those like him. Thus, love is a destabilizing force in relation to ego structures of family, ethnicity, nationality, capital. But, this does not meant that love then abandons the project of material transformation. Material transformation is still a priority for S, yet it is one that is grounded in the expansive and inclusive ideal of love that embraces otherness. In fact, this love directs his desire very specifically to an outside that lacks material comfort and material power. Love is directed in a renewing and transforming way, embracing the forces of change, in order to demand that the basic material and emotional needs of those rejected by the ego structures are met.

S believes, then, that what we need for redemption to occur in this world is not activity oriented toward preserving structures that keep us bound in our little worlds of righteousness and purity, but we need a great big love.

> *great big love*
> *sweeping across the sky*[24]

The thing about a great big love is that it leads S to work for change in the world but does not allow him to become attached to the ideal of perfection, to the idea that he personally is responsible for changing everything into perfection. Great big love represents an ability that S is acquiring to live with both the bad and the good, fighting the bad without developing, as happens so often with those working for change, a self-righteous attitude towards those perceived to be perpetuating the bad.

> *seen a lot of things in the world outside*
> *some bad but some good stuff too*
> *felt the touch of love in the works of God*
> *and now and then in what people do*
> *never had a lot of faith in human beings*

> *but sometimes we manage to shine*
> *like a light on a hill beaming out to space*
> *from somewhere hard to find* [25]

This orientation establishes the elsewhere of great big love. Love is there to renew in those places in need of renewal, but also is absent, meaning that love is not fully expressed there or at any one moment or place, but as the ideal, is bigger than anything we have experienced or done so far. Thus, S becomes convinced that he must work for the good but, at the same time, realizes that the good is always still in a process of realization, is not yet, is still elsewhere as well as present.

The elsewhere presence of great big love is one that is captured by the wind and the forces associated with the wind.

> *I love the pounding of hooves*
> *I love engines that roar*
> *I love the wild music of waves on the shore*
> *and the spiral perfection of a hawk when it soars*
> *love my sweet woman down to the core* [26]

There are lots of roads that S can travel. Earth roads working for justice. And spirit roads working for enlightenment of the spirit. Whichever roads he travels S understands that these roads are always uncertain, and their very uncertainty is what makes them pleasurable.

> *there's roads and there's roads*
> *and they call, can't you hear it?*
> *roads of the earth*
> *and roads of the spirit*

the best roads of all
are the ones that aren't certain
one those is where you'll find me
till they drop the big curtain [27]

The best roads are the ones pushed by the wind, the light wind, the cool breeze, bringing release and expansion. S is then released from his troubles to be captured by the expansive sky and the paternal embrace of the diamond light, an inclusive Christ-love of everything that lives, a love of a good father for the child. And, as if affirming Christ's wisdom, S understands that, no matter how old he is, he needs to become like a child again to experience renewal.

hear the wind moan
in the bright diamond sky
these mountains are waiting
brown-green and dry
I'm too old for the term
but I'll use it anyway
I'll be a child of the wind
till the end of my days [28]

In order to discover redemption, S needs to discover laughter, a unique laughter. He know knows that he should avoid the laughter that comes from pleasures of ego-attachments:

it's not the laughter you can hide behind
it's not the laughter of a frightened mind
it's not the laughter of the macho fool
it's not the laughter that obeys the rules [29]

Rather,

> *you better listen to the laugh of love* [30]

Redemptive laughter is the laugh of love and it comes when he is

> *balanced on the brink only waiting for a shove* [31]

Removing himself from the everyday securities that prevent him from opening up to the outside, S sits on the edge of a cliff looking out on to the expanse, understanding that whatever might happen to him, he is contained and held by a love that is everywhere and anywhere, and that he can, with ecstatic abandon, open himself up to that expanse.

> *everybody's looking for who they are* [32]

Everybody's searching for answers, for a redemptive knowledge of self. Where can this be found?

> *could be the famine*
> *could be the feast*
> *cold be the pusher*
> *could be the priest* [33]

S knows that he could possibly be subjected to a range of emotional and material experiences in life. He could experience hunger and famine. Or he could experience abundance and continual feasting. These experiences come to people irrespective of rank and status, both drug pushers and religious priests. Thus, it is not these kind of oppositions that pose the problem for S in his quest for redemption. Redemption will not come at a material level by opposing famine to feast. It will not come by claiming that all will be well when we overcome the problems of hunger and provide material abundance for all. Redemption will not come at a moral level by playing off morally corrupt individuals like drug pushers to the moral purity of the religious priest. The problem for redemption is a lack of love:

it's always ourselves we love the least [34]

Whether he goes hungry or whether he is able to feast, whether he pushes drugs or whether he preach and performs the sacraments, in any and all cases, the real question for S is whether, in his various and diverse life-experiences, there is love.

that's the burden of the angel/beast [35]

Love does not discriminate according to the neat moral categories his ego-self might set up to tie down or nail down the contours of paradise. Love can take the form of an angel or a beast and it is not the presence of angel or beast that is important, but the presence of love. This has been hard for S to understand, given his attachment to the binaries of ego thinking:

we go crying, we come laughing
never understand the time we're passing [36]

S doesn't understand the suffering that occurs in the world, when everything seems to go wrong. But he can identify with it:

when the wild-eyed dogs of day to day
come snapping at your heels
and there's so much coming at you
that you don't know how to feel

when they've taken all your money
and then come back for you clothes
when your hands are full of thorns
but you can't quit groping for the rose [37]

In full identification with the troubles, S understands that he cannot fix it all, that he cannot completely wipe out the objective manifestations of the pain and misery. But he does know that what he can do is provide love:

in the southland of the heart
where night blooms perfume the breeze
lie down
take your rest with me [38]

When he encounters someone who is suffering, whose heart is heavy with the burdens of existence, then in the restfulness of the night, when a light wind can displace the heaviness of the day, when a cool breeze can bring relief, then as a friend and lover S will offer up the tenderness of his touch. And not just to those like him, those he knows well, but also to the stranger who crosses his path. He especially needs to invite into his embrace those who suffer so much emotionally, who experience all those awful thoughts that torment them, who feel the burden of traumatic memories, both done and done to, who wake up to the new day with a heaviness and an exhaustion that is incapacitating:

when thoughts you've tried to leave behind
keep sniping from the dark
when the fire burns inside you but
you jump from every spark
when your heart's beset by memories

you wish you'd never made
when the sun comes up an enemy, and nothing gives you shade
in the southland of the heart
where the saints go lazily
take your rest with me [39]

S slips out of town at night, hopping a train

not a knife throw from here you can hear the night train passing
that's the sound somebody makes when they're getting away [40]

in order to flee the pain of life, the horror of life, the constant and ever-present violence.

leaving next week's hanging jury far behind them
prisoner of the choices they have made [41]

He is burdened by all those bad choices which take on a condemning voice ringing in his head, judging, judging.

ice cube in a dark drink shines like star light
the moon is floating somewhere out at sea [42]

It is to the darkness that S turns for solace. He submerges himself in the dark liquid, hoping to forget his troubles. Yet, as he is surrounded by the darkness he catches hold of an ice cube that reflects the moon light and becomes a star of redemption.

on an island in the blur of noise and colour [43]

The dark liquid, aided by the light reflected off the ice cube, has carried him to an island refuge. His drink has become a temporary sanctuary from the pain and misery of life.

and everyone's an island edged with sand
a temporary refuge where somebody else can stand [44]

It is from this island refuge and sanctuary that is a good distance from the troubles of his life that S is able to create an open and inviting space of care and concern, a space of love, for other who similarly need relief from the storm of life.

> *till the sea that binds us like the forced tie of a blood oath*
> *will wear it down, dissolve it, recombine it* [45]

The island must not, though, become a prison, where the refuge becomes a bunker, with high brick walls to protect us from any intrusion from the outside. S understands that he must be able to continually give up the island at the very same time as create it, subject himself to a constant to and fro movement, where he creates a refuge from the trouble, but then gives up that space again to the sea, allowing the sea to dissolve the trouble, so that any movement of island-refuge toward ego-structure, fearful of the other, is thwarted, so that the space of sanctuary can again form in another space and time of trouble.

> *anyone can die here they do it every day*
> *it doesn't take much effort though it goes against the grain*
> *and the ultimate forgetfulness of violence*
> *sweeps the landscape like a headlight of a train* [46]

In the face of the constant violence which so overwhelms the global landscape, the only recourse for S is to hop on to the night train which will relentlessly carry us away. The headlight of the train, as a light of redemption, does not cure the violence, but instead allows for S a forgetfulness of the violence. The light sweeps over all the trouble out there, not to transform it into objective, material paradise, but instead to wash the trouble clean from his memory. The train then moves on, and those memories which haunt S are passed by.

> *ice cube in a dark drink shines like star light*
> *starlight shines like shards in dark hair*
> *and the mind's eye tumbles out along the steel track*
> *fixing every shadow with its stare* [47]

As he holds his drink sitting by the window of the train, as the train speeds through farm and village, as he alternates his gaze from the drink to the landscape outside, S has a vision that the light of redemption comes through shards of glass, which do not concentrate the light in a coherent vision of transformation, but disperses the light through the darkness, giving us moments of ecstasy, moments of peace and reconciliation, but nothing in the way of a full revelation of paradise. Here, S displays a pessimism or distrust concerning any coherent vision of transformation or any full revelation of paradise. His hard-won insight is that, in the face of the violence and horror, any vision or revelation that is coherent and full, in terms of a program and an agenda, makes a mockery of the pain and misery that is suffered, offering candy-coated illusions about our ability to change all this. Maybe it is better simply to forget, to not search in the passing memories for signs of paradise, but to with steely eyes stare down the evil, and then move on.

> *and in the absence of a vision there are nightmares*
> *and in the absence of compassion there is cancer*
> *whose banner waves over palaces and mean streets*
> *and the rhythm of the night train is a mantra* [48]

On the night train there is no vision to change the world, only the presence of nightmares which need to be forgotten. When he looks out on the social landscape that passes, to the world of grinding poverty for so many, to the world of ethnic cleansing and mass graves, to the world of gloating rich building more elaborate and luxurious palaces, contemptuous of the abuses that come when people outside the gates are constantly beaten down on mean streets, then S wonders where the compassion really is in this world, when all he sees is cancer. The only response is to stay on the train and let it take us somewhere else.

> *sunset is an angel weeping*
> *holding out a bloody sword*
> *no matter how I squint I cannot*
> *make out what it's pointing toward*
> *sometimes you feel like you live too long*
> *days dripping slowly on the page*
> *you catch yourself*
> *pacing the cage* [49]

S is having a difficult time figuring out the vision of the angel in terms of the coming of paradise. Seems more now like an angel weeping, only holding out the sword of violence to those who want to end the pain and the suffering. He finds himself exhausted when he thinks about the action needed in the struggle against injustice and oppression Exhausted when he thinks about trying to realize paradise here in this messed up world. The struggle now seems meaningless, the action simply a repetition of action, a pacing of the cage. Before, he was so confident about the ability of symbolic projects to transform for the good. Now, these symbolic projects look like a constant return to the starting point, a move forward and then backward.

> *I've proven who I am so many times*
> *the magnetic strip's worn thin*
> *and each time I was someone else*
> *and everyone was taken in*
> *hours chatter in high places*
> *stir up eddies in the dust of rage*
> *set me to pacing the cage* [50]

As S moved from the tight circle of love to a wider symbolic action in the world it seemed possible to find a meaningful identity in those projects. That he could find solutions through proving himself in the world outside the safe country home, could find an identity there. And this was not a fixed identity, either. S realized that the identity he strove for was one that needed to be open to the other, that identity was affirmed in an intersubjective space of love, was changing all the time with the various options provided by the symbolic. Now, this project of intersubjective identity based on the ground of love seems an illusion to be overcome. That in the last instance spirit moves forward not progressively, but through the mantra-like movement of pacing back and forth, back and forth. That enlightenment comes more from an awareness of the fact of pacing rather than a progressive movement toward paradise.

> *I never knew what you all wanted*
> *so I gave you everything*
> *all that I could pillage*
> *all the spells that I could sing*

it's as if the thing were written
in the constitution of the age
sooner or later you'll wind up
pacing the cage [51]

In his earlier affirmative movement out to the other, S was trying
to please the other through his attachment to symbolic projects,
a symbolic movement of identity masks. But now he believes that
redemption does not come through pleasing the other in this
way, that in the end you will be left pacing.

sometimes the best map will not guide you
you can't see what's round the bend
sometimes the road leads through dark places
sometimes the darkness is your friend
today these eyes scan bleached-out land
for the coming of the outbound stage
pacing the cage [52]

In the end the symbolic maps to paradise are worthless. The
cause of the world is not the progressive move toward paradise
but the constant unbinding of everything. This is what is most
real. If the real as cause is unbound, then we should attempt to
subjectify the cause, internalize the real unbound as cause.

I woke up thinking about Turkish drummers
it didn't take long: I don't know much about Turkish drummers
but it made me think of Germany
and the guy who sold me cigarettes
who'd been in the Afghan secret police
who'd made the observation
that it's hard…to live [53]

Thinking about drummers, cigarettes, restaurants. A free
association, a metonymic travel, a symbolic work. All which covers
up the trauma of the real which is better captured in the image of
the secret police. Movement from sign to sign in avoidance of the
violence committed. Realization of a primordial always already
fallenness to the love that was in the beginning. The symbolic
work of transformation has, in the past, been directed against the
material fallenness from a love that was there in the beginning.
Now, rather than a fallenness from love, S is aware of a fallenness
inherent to love which has not, up to this point, been subjectified.

> *somebody stands at a window*
> *watches the river roll*
> *trains tumble in the foreground*
> *with the weight of approaching dawn* [54]

The river of death rolls on. The train of death rolls on. The
trauma of death rolls on.

> *flames from the refinery, rise broken-red and riveting*
> *and the high vault of heaven, looks far away and cold* [55]

The death of fire comes where heaven seems very far way.

> *there's a howling in the factory yard*
> *there's a pounding in my head* [56]

All is falling apart. All the great symbolic attempts to redeem in
ruin. And all S is left with is a pounding in the head, like a
mantra, like the relentless movement of the train.

> *I'm swollen up with unshed tears*
> *bloated like the dead* [57]

Swollen, bloated, dead to active life.

get up Jonah
it's your time to be born [58]

Don't see this all as fate. Subjectify the cause and pass through it. Get up to be born the subject of faith. But what does it mean to be a subject of faith that has passed through death? What does it mean to engage fully in a process of identification with pain and destitution so that a transformation occurs, a new birth into a new subjectivity?

Our reborn subject turns once again to the prophetic tradition. He will be like Jonah. Jonah was vomited from the belly of the fish to proclaim to the city of Ninevah that the injustice and oppression rife in that great city had to stop. Ninevah would be destroyed unless there was a movement towards material and spiritual renewal. Our reborn subject must likewise go out into the world as a prophet to loudly proclaim that if things are not changed, if the violence and abuse and hunger is not corrected then the whole thing is going to be destroyed.

To get up as Jonah, to be reborn as a subject is, then, not to succumb to the death in an escapism or a mystical indifference, but to go out boldly and announce that what is does not constitute paradise and must immediately undergo monumental changes to forestall a final act of destruction and apocalypse. There isn't much time: Get up Jonah.

NOTES

1. The interpretation of this third moment of S is inspired by Julia Kristeva's *Strangers To Ourselves*. Trans. Leon S. Roudiez. Columbia Univ. Press, 1991, and *Nations Without Nationalism*. Trans. Leon S. Roudiez. Columbia Univ. Press, 1993. Also, as the interpretation again approaches Lacan, especially around the idea of subject as cause, see Bruce Fink. *The Lacanian Subject*. Princeton University Press, 1995.

2. "Shipwrecked at the Stable Door," *Big Circumstance*.

3. Ibid.

4. Ibid.

5. Ibid.

6. Ibid.

7. "Gospel of Bondage," *Big Circumstance*.

8. Ibid.

9. Ibid.

10. Ibid.

11. Ibid.

12. "Understanding Nothing," *Big Circumstance*.

13. Ibid.

14. "Where the Death Squad Lives," *Big Circumstance*.

15. Ibid.

16. Ibid.

17. Ibid.

18. Ibid.

19. "Mighty Trucks of Midnight," *Nothing But a Burning Light*.

20. Ibid.

21. Ibid.

22. Ibid.

23. Ibid.

24. "Great Big Love," *Nothing But a Burning Light*.

25. Ibid.

26. "Child of the Wind," *Nothing But a Burning Light*.

27. Ibid.

28. Ibid.
29. "Listen For the Laugh," *Dart to the Heart.*
30. Ibid.
31. Ibid.
32. "Burden of the Angel/Beast," *Dart to the Heart.*
33. Ibid.
34. Ibid.
35. Ibid.
36. Ibid.
37. "Southland of the Heart," *Dart to the Heart.*
38. Ibid.
39. Ibid.
40. "Night Train," *Charity of Night.*
41. Ibid.
42. Ibid.
43. Ibid.
44. Ibid.
45. Ibid.
46. Ibid.
47. bid.
48. Ibid.
49. "Pacing the Cage," *Charity of Night.*
50. Ibid.
51. Ibid.
52. Ibid.
53. "Get Up Jonah," *Charity of Night.*
54. Ibid.
55. Ibid.
56. Ibid.
57. Ibid.
58. Ibid.

Conclusion

I and S Together, Apart

This book has engaged in a series of reflections on the work of Leonard Cohen and Bruce Cockburn. It has proposed two subjects, I from Cohen's work, and S from Cockburn's work. These two subjects have each experienced a journey of desire in which persistent themes have emerged. The following involves some concluding reflections on some of those themes.

Concerning origins, the original, the primary, I's experience points to an always already ruined original. This state of being always already ruined does not restrict the possibilities for I's desire, but becomes the (un)ground for the freedom and creativity of his desire. In the beginning there is no stable presence for subjectivity, and therefore the substance of subjectivity is centered on a nothingness, absence, emptiness, the hole. Proceeding in time, all later pursuits fall under the sign of this originary nothingness or emptiness, meaning that any pursuit is bound to come to pieces, or better, is unbound and unraveled.

Because desire is always already deconstructed, never had a chance, there is no possibility in I's experience for a social-material restoration, or, there is a restoration, but it is a restoration of a primary lack, which doesn't fit the usual models of social-material restoration. Redemption, where structures of love are created that provide the ground for freedom, is an imaginary illusion, a kind of sleep or trance to be awakened from. These structures only trap and bind masculine desire, leading eventually to unfreedom.

The relationship of S to origins is somewhat different. For S, there is an originally good creation, which exists as a set of potentials to be realized. These are potentials for structures of love to be created by human activity in space and time, structures that would provide a holding environment for the free desire of the subject. Freedom is here understood as always taking place within social-material structures that make concerted, determined and creative action in the world possible. Yet, the structures that are created in social-material space and time are not always structures of love allowing freedom, not always developments of the potential there in the beginning. Many times these structures become ego-traps that bind masculine desire. In short, social-material structures can become forms of idolatry that are worshiped for their own sake, with subjects bowing to the gods of security and safety, leading to a stifling of desire, to unfreedom. This is what S believes to be evil. It is what he believes leads to forms of injustice in social-material space and time.

Structures of love are created not through the fixing of desire in secure borders and boundaries, but through establishing frameworks of intersubjectivity, the activity of subjects reciprocally recognizing each other's independence and freedom, recognizing each other's difference, establishing a big space for the entertaining of diversity.

Yet, according to S, the evil of idolatry seems to prevail in our world presently. In the search for security, for control and mastery, for protection from the dangerous outside where the dominance of the same prevails, subjects create bordered walls of nationality, ethnicity, familial homogeneity, sexual conformism, and learn to hate that which falls outside those walls, indeed, are driven to destroy the outside of difference.

Maybe, in the end, what is needed is the apocalypse, a colossal burning of all this evil, in order for it to be possible that structures which promote the good can reappear?

Concerning questions of gender and difference, I's experience reveals the maternal as an imaginary trap, a love that consumes and suffocates, a great mother that squelches the freedom of desire. Movement beyond the imaginary trap of the maternal takes place through the access to the symbolic paternal which draws upon the power of the always already ruined state of being to continually unravel the weaving of the maternal web. The symbolic paternal draws on the strength of the superego as death drive, which loves to go after the imaginary ego of subjects drawn into the maternal web.

At the same time, I's journey shows that real access to freedom and redemption of desire occurs not through the symbolic paternal, but through access to a higher feminine state, a higher state of the death drive, the ultimate nothingness and loss of the great goddess. She is the great loser, and it is only losers who receive redemption, it is only losers who are able to draw on the power of the always already state of ruin that is the real power in the world.

I, as a loser, is thus placed in a unique position with respect to the feminine other. He is allowed access to an other *jouissance*, a pleasure beyond imaginary and symbolic pleasure which is ego-bound. This establishes the feminine as veiled, a pleasure in nothingness, a pleasure in the ruin. Yet, I is also granted the presence of the angel, who holds him in the midst of the ruin. And it is the presence of the angel that shows us that, in the end, I still seeks to be held, still seeks a love structure of a sort. In this sense, compassion, as given by the angel, is not illusory, an avoidance of the truth, but in communion with the ruin, the ultimate in love.

For S, the maternal is, in the beginning, good. It is not always already ruined, but provides a space that holds as S prepares to move out with confidence into the world of activity and creativity. Originally, the maternal space is not closed, not suffocating, but open and accepting of difference and diversity. Moreover, in time, it continually expands outwards, the circle getting bigger and bigger, embracing more and more difference and diversity. The paternal is a metaphor for this expansion of the maternal space outwards, becoming a loving father, who holds at the same time as encourages free movement.

And as the space of desire expands outwards, S as an active subject is able to meet the feminine other as a recognized subject. The influence of the loving father is one that encourages S to recognize the feminine other as subject. The expanded space thus becomes a great big love that is grounded not in walls and borders that fear and, possibly, hate the other, but in intersubjective recognition. This generates a distinctive ecstasy of two subjects recognizing and affirming each other as good. Here, contact with the feminine other brings compassion for S, compassion in a world that is, outside the structures of love created, a world that is in ruin. However, the compassion that S receives from the feminine other is not in communion with the ruin, but in defiance of the ruin, understanding this ruin not as the always already beginning, but as an evil departure from the beginning. The compassion that he receives in the space of love is one that can energize him to get up and fight against evil, before it is too late.

Yet, although the paths of masculine desire for I and S are different, they are similar to the extent that they both seek to maintain a dialectical tension between *the present* and *paradise*. For both I and S, it is vitally important that these two not be conflated. In this sense, the present conditions of existence do not reflect the true potential for paradise and must be critiqued for not doing so. At the same time, however, the present conditions of existence do express and do embody, in some form, paradise, and it is also the duty of the artist to portray the forms in which paradise appears.

The reason that both Leonard Cohen and Bruce Cockburn's work is successful and appealing is that each of them is able to bring these two sides of the dialectic together. The task in successful dialectical expression is not to, at one moment, express the separation of the present and paradise, then at the next moment, express their connection, but to be able to present images that are able to convey both poles at the same time, with the sublation of both occurring continuously and instantaneously.

Leonard Cohen's work, through the subject I, performs this dialectical tension between the present and paradise in a deconstructive manner. Paradise announces itself through the activity of destroying the present forms of the masculine ego, present forms that prevent this announcement. And it is in the space left open by the symbolic destruction of the phallus that the eternal feminine can bring happiness and contentment. Yet, even though present symbolic activity is needed to allow paradise to be experienced, masculine desire is fooled when it conflates the symbolic with the real, when it conflates the present activity with paradise itself. This is why the mystical presence of the feminine angel is so important. Being granted her presence allows I the conviction that paradise is always other to present, active expressions, even though we only gain awareness of it through that activity in the here and now.

Bruce Cockburn's work, through the subject S, also performs the dialectical tension between the present and paradise deconstructively. It is the task of the prophet-poet to demonstrate, not just at home, in the familiar, but everywhere in the world, in all that may be unfamiliar, the extent to which the idols of ego-power, although often believed to be an expression of paradise, often do not live up to its demands. Paradise is not here, not in these present expressions where social-material inequality is so evident, is other to them. Yet, paradise is here, is in those very present expressions where justice is absent, and therefore is not other to them. For the presence of love finds expression at the moment love seems to have escaped the world. This is why, for Cockburn, the imagery of apocalypse, expressed in *Night Vision*, is so important. Apocalyptic images convey the essence of the dialectic: Everything is falling apart, yet love rules.

CONCLUSION

Paradise present, but not present. The work of Leonard Cohen and Bruce Cockburn presents us with a dialectical image of masculine desire, one that brings together, without unifying, the sentiments of a Judaic tradition of masculine desire and a Christian tradition of masculine desire.

And if I may end on a personal note (I now referring not to the I of Cohen's work, but the I of Nonnekes), with specific reference to the dedication of this book to my father, a Dutch Reformed pastor whose life-work was defined by both Judaic and Christian sentiments, I wish to say that, having been raised in this Dutch Reformed tradition, and now informed by the encounter with Cohen and Cockburn, I have arrived at a post-ecclesiastical vision of masculine desire. I believe in paradise, and am attracted to images of paradise coming from the past, from tradition, while at the same time I possess an inability, unwillingness, and determined commitment not to believe in the images presented from the past and by tradition, especially those held in an exclusive manner. This, it seems, has left me in a quandary, but it is a dialectical quandary, and one that I am quite satisfied with, a satisfaction that can only come through what, in the end, is an image-less encounter with the real.

Index

abandonment, 122, 146

absence, 146, 147, 150, 165, 173

absence, 4, 8, 23, 39, 58, 64, 65, 76, 80, 99, 101, 102, 104, 105, 112, 113, 115-117, 127

abstraction, 116, 117

active subject, 10, 85, 86, 124, 176

aggression, 17, 75, 80, 83-85

ambivalence, 101, 102, 112

Amos, 80, 135-137

angel, 4, 5, 9, 36, 43-47, 84, 103, 106, 161, 166, 172, 176, 178

anger, 79-82, 94, 100, 124

anxiety, 51, 62, 76, 79, 101, 103, 104, 106, 107, 112, 116, 117

apocalypse, 79, 81, 170, 175, 178

aura, 38-40, 42, 46, 108

authentic, 7, 39, 44-46

baptism, 27, 28

becoming, 19, 23, 28, 38, 105, 130

big circumstance, 8, 147, 148

birds, 52, 58, 69

blood, 22, 29, 82, 120, 121, 134, 139, 164, 166

boat, 75, 85

brain, 22, 23, 31, 32

breeze, 43, 44, 60, 61, 79, 81, 159, 162

brokenness, 96, 121, 153

burning, 37, 59, 60, 76, 132, 133, 175

cage, 166-168

Catherine Tekakwitha, 4, 22, 26, 27, 33

cause, the, 78, 79, 133, 168, 170

celebration, 5, 62, 67, 130

child, 8, 16, 23, 60, 65, 111, 119, 120, 121, 137, 159

Christ, 5, 28, 33, 62, 71, 72, 85, 116, 159, 179

Christianity, 5, 7, 22, 116, 179

circle of doom, 72, 73, 75

INDEX

circle of love, 65, 72, 73, 75, 92, 93, 99, 106, 110, 119-122, 167

city, 46, 51, 102, 107-109, 111, 112, 170

clouds, 56-58, 113

commodity, 38, 67, 68, 111

community, 93-95, 105, 111, 116, 118, 120, 137, 141, 149

consumption, 39

contact, 21, 26, 32, 41, 68, 70, 113, 128, 130, 131, 177

container, 10, 70, 101, 112

containing, 55, 112, 119

containment, 51, 104, 112, 113, 115, 147

contentment, 45, 112, 113, 178

control, 16, 20, 25, 37, 41, 42, 45, 98, 120, 127, 155, 175

covenant, 135-137

creator, 59

critique, 7, 65, 75, 129, 135-137, 154

crowd, the, 28, 29, 45, 69, 95, 126

cut, 15, 22, 67, 72, 82, 87, 101, 106, 109, 111, 126-128, 130, 150, 151

daddy, 15, 72

dancing, 47, 85, 86, 133

darkness, 52, 55, 56, 71, 76-79, 83, 85, 92, 117, 138, 139, 142, 151, 163, 168

day dream, 99

death, 17, 19, 20, 23, 31, 33, 34, 38-40, 42, 45-47, 64, 71-75, 79-82, 108, 117, 151, 153, 169, 170, 175

death drive, 19, 20, 40, 42, 147, 151, 156, 175

devil, 66-68

dialectic, 3, 7, 96, 117, 177-179

diamonds, 67, 68, 139, 140

difference, 4, 8, 16, 22, 31, 72, 81, 95, 106, 118, 120, 122, 156, 175, 176

displacement, 2, 77, 103

divine, 84, 86, 87, 92, 110, 124, 125, 128, 135, 136, 141, 146

dreaming, 60, 63, 64

ecstasy, 21, 26, 34, 68, 93, 101, 109, 110, 112-114, 165, 177

ego, 3, 4, 17, 19, 20, 23, 32, 39, 40, 45, 46, 54, 55, 67, 68, 71-73, 95, 98, 106, 116, 117, 119-123, 127, 129-131, 137, 147, 148, 151, 153-157, 159, 161, 164, 174-176, 178

emptiness, 18, 23, 25, 32, 47, 173, 174

enlightenment, 3, 4, 11, 39, 92, 158, 167

evil, 11, 60, 65-68, 72-76, 78, 80-83, 86, 87, 94-96, 99, 100, 102, 105, 114, 116, 117, 119-121, 123, 133, 140, 141, 147, 148, 151-153, 165, 174, 175, 177

fall, 26, 65, 71, 107

fantasy, 16, 32, 95, 126, 127

father, imaginary, 72, 98, 101, 103, 104, 112, 119-121, 176

father, loving, 8, 12, 51, 61, 65, 85, 88

father, oedipal, 98, 103, 128

father, superego, 117, 120, 121

father, symbolic, 21, 28

fear, 31, 84, 96-98, 105, 155, 164, 176

feminine, 4, 5, 9, 10, 18, 25, 26, 28-32, 36, 37-40, 42-44, 46, 60, 61, 103, 120, 130, 131, 175-178

fragmentation, 46, 125, 127

friend-lover, 110

glass, 27, 55, 70, 71, 165

God, 53, 69, 80, 87, 88, 102, 103, 123, 124, 135-137, 150, 152, 157

goddess, 4, 18, 26-28, 33, 175
gospel of bondage, 150, 151, 153, 154
grace, 78, 107, 156
great mother, 22, 25, 26, 32, 33, 175

happiness, 67, 72, 136, 137, 156, 178
hate, 98-100, 125, 133, 137, 175, 176
heaven, 22, 23, 44, 59, 73, 83, 87, 118, 138, 169
helplessness, 100, 101
hidden, 43, 55, 67, 139
horror, 5, 8, 20, 41, 42, 44, 46, 47, 133, 140, 163, 165
hysteria, 16

ideal, 2, 3, 6-10, 21, 62, 72, 74-76, 78, 84, 93, 94, 96, 114, 116, 118, 124, 157, 158
identification, 9, 33, 52, 61-67, 71, 84, 104, 106, 116, 122, 123, 150, 162, 170
idolatry, 123, 136, 137, 146, 148, 174, 175
idols, 17, 55, 67, 72, 129, 136, 151, 178
imaginary, the, 4, 12, 15, 16, 17, 19, 20, 22, 23, 25, 26, 28, 30, 32, 34, 85, 95, 106, 109, 174-176
intersubjective, 7, 65, 69, 72, 80, 93, 95, 99, 100, 104, 106, 111, 113-117, 122, 124, 130, 165, 176
intersubjectivity, 93, 95, 113, 116, 175
island, 163, 164

jewels, 67, 68
Jonah, 170
jouissance, 17, 20, 29, 32, 39, 40, 42, 45, 55, 68, 176
joy, 74, 86
justice, 5, 6, 11, 60, 93, 114, 115, 117-119, 123, 124, 135-137, 139, 141, 147, 155, 158, 178

lack, 10, 21-23, 73, 80, 99, 100, 112, 117, 133, 139, 153, 154, 157, 161, 174
language, 16, 17, 20, 28, 61-64, 71, 102, 128, 133, 146, 147, 149
laughter, 65, 83, 113, 159, 160
law, 31, 66, 135
lightness, 52, 58, 79
lily, 138-141
loneliness, 16, 18, 26, 28, 31, 34, 97, 98, 122, 134
lonely, 21, 26, 28, 32, 34, 41, 56, 93, 98, 122
loner, 121-124
loser, 2-4, 33, 175, 176

madness, 30, 32
magic, 31, 45
Mary, 28, 33, 84, 56, 77, 97, 101, 112, 127, 128, 173, 174
mask, 45, 46, 168
masochism, 17, 20
mass, the, 39, 45, 46, 48
mastery, 25, 45, 98, 120, 155, 175
maternal, 9, 10, 15-17, 21, 22, 25, 26, 28, 30, 32-34, 52, 54, 57, 60, 61, 63, 68, 69, 87, 101, 103, 105, 110, 112, 119, 120, 131, 132, 136, 146, 175, 176
melancholic, 65
melancholy, 64, 66
metaphor, 2, 77, 153, 176
metaphorical, 77, 112
metonymic, 77, 103, 169
metonymy, 2, 77
mirror, 36, 37, 41, 51, 52, 55-57, 139
moon, 32, 57, 113, 130, 131, 138-140, 163
morning, 56-58, 86, 134, 141

narcissism, 16, 17, 28, 93, 137
nationalism, 28, 155, 171

INDEX

natural, 8, 51, 69, 93, 111, 114

nature, 5, 8, 52, 53, 55, 57, 59, 63-65, 72, 73, 79, 102, 104, 111, 123

negation, 123, 124

night, 41, 57, 74, 85, 87, 108, 109, 113, 130-133, 138-141, 154, 155, 162-166, 171

nightmares, 165, 166

normal, 86, 123, 124, 129, 146

nothingness, 3, 4, 7, 8, 21, 23, 25, 28, 43, 47, 122, 124, 150, 151, 173-176

now-time, 2, 127

nurturance, 52, 58, 63

nurture, 55, 61

nurturing, 16, 93, 116

omnipotence, 95, 99

oppression, 122, 124, 133, 135, 137, 138, 141, 148, 153, 166, 170

ordinary eternal machinery, 15, 18, 20, 25, 32, 36

original, 3, 77, 97, 101-106, 112, 119, 126-128, 173, 174, 176

other, 3, 5, 9-11, 22, 25, 36-39, 41-43, 46, 51, 54, 57, 61, 63, 64, 66, 67, 76, 95, 98, 102, 105-107, 109, 111, 113, 116-120, 124, 130, 136, 137, 140, 142, 149, 150, 151, 153, 155-157, 164, 167, 168, 175, 176-178

outside, 16, 28, 54, 60, 61, 74, 75, 80, 84, 92, 102, 105-108, 116-118, 120-124, 128, 129, 131, 137, 148-150, 155-157, 160, 164-167, 175, 177

outsider, 121, 123, 148, 149, 155

pain, 8, 17-19, 23, 33, 34, 73, 74, 94-96, 98, 100-102, 105, 106, 109, 110, 113, 114, 116, 118, 120-122, 130, 151, 162, 163, 165, 166, 170

paradise, 6-8, 41, 44, 45, 66, 79, 84, 94, 121, 123-125, 128-132, 141, 142, 146-149, 151, 153, 155, 161, 164-168, 170, 177-179

paradox, 115, 116, 118, 172

paternal, 9, 10, 27, 28, 52, 54, 55, 57, 59-61, 63, 66, 68, 69, 71, 72, 77, 84, 101, 103, 105, 110, 112, 117, 119-121, 131, 136, 146, 159, 175, 176

perfection, 152, 157, 158

pessimism, 87, 148, 165

phallic, 4, 18, 21, 25-27, 30, 32, 66, 87

phallus, 15, 17, 27, 34, 40, 43, 178

pleasure, 18-20, 22, 44-46, 67, 68, 159, 176

poetic, 9, 10, 38-40, 42, 46, 47, 53, 63, 64, 66, 86, 102, 128, 129, 132, 147

political, 5, 7, 8, 11, 28, 32, 76

politics, 32, 65, 123

potentials, 119, 174

power, 4, 18, 20, 36, 37, 40, 43, 59, 62, 65, 66, 71-76, 78, 80-82, 85, 86, 95, 109, 122, 129, 132, 134-140, 148, 149, 154, 157, 175, 176, 178

prophetic voice, 129, 130, 135

protection, 37, 51, 52, 65, 112, 113, 115, 132, 175

rainbow, 66, 70, 139

real, the, 4, 16, 17, 23, 26, 28, 32-34, 37, 42-45, 168, 169, 178, 179

recognition, 41, 52, 80, 93-95, 111, 114-117, 120, 122, 130, 177

redemption, 9, 23, 25, 26, 28, 31, 32, 41, 42, 46, 47, 66-68, 70, 71, 73, 82, 83, 116, 121, 122, 131, 132, 137, 138, 142, 149, 152, 157, 159-161, 163-165, 174-176

renewal, 132, 138, 139, 149, 151, 158, 159, 170

repression, 22, 123

restoration, 135, 137, 174

revolution, 6, 75, 83, 133, 134, 137, 138

roads, 158, 159

rock, 27, 67, 68, 141

rules, 20, 30, 79, 129, 159, 178

sadness, 97, 98

sameness, 28, 95

Satan, 71, 72

sea, 8, 43, 54, 55, 59, 63, 68-70, 72, 73, 75, 79, 81, 83-86, 99, 102, 106, 113, 114, 119, 126, 163, 164

security, 3, 17, 27, 30, 47, 54, 56-58, 63, 84, 96, 104, 106, 123, 124, 155, 174, 175

ship, 69

shipwrecked, 145, 149

sky, 32, 52, 55-59, 64, 67-70, 77, 79, 84, 85, 87, 102, 108, 132, 138, 140, 157, 159

space, 10, 18, 19, 21, 37, 51, 58, 59, 68-70, 76, 78, 81, 101, 102, 104, 108, 118, 119, 121, 122, 125-128, 139-141, 146, 158, 164, 167, 174-178

speech, 26, 61, 62

spirit, 9, 23, 25, 32, 52, 58, 68-70, 72, 76, 77, 79, 80, 87, 99, 104, 109, 111, 113, 115, 116, 130, 131, 148, 150, 153, 158, 167

splitting, 71-73, 79, 84, 86

storm, 30, 55-57, 61, 96, 128, 164

strangeness, 102, 119

subjectivity, 23, 32, 45, 46, 78, 85, 86, 95, 108, 121, 122, 128, 170, 173

sun, 8, 51-63, 65-70, 73, 75, 79-82, 84, 86, 99, 102-104, 106, 114, 119, 125, 130-132, 138-140, 142, 163, 166

sun dance, 130, 131

superego, 72, 98, 116, 117, 120, 121, 127, 175

symbolic, the, 4, 8, 9, 15-20, 22, 23, 25-28, 30-34, 39-46, 52, 62, 69, 129, 146, 149-152, 155, 166-169, 175, 176, 178

symbols, 21, 32, 123, 128

systems, 26, 32, 43, 103, 120, 150, 152

transitional space, 69, 139-141

tavern, 46, 47, 107

telephone dance, 15, 20, 23, 24

train, 82, 103, 147, 163-166, 169

transcendence, 60

transcendent, 62, 67

transference, 130

transferential, 61, 62

trauma, 81, 162, 169

traveling, 56, 77, 92, 95, 103

uncanny, 43, 45

unity, 29, 93-95, 101, 105, 111, 113, 116, 118, 120, 126, 137, 141, 149

veil, 25, 28, 29, 31, 32, 36, 42, 43, 48, 176

violence, 17, 40, 41, 65, 133, 134, 140, 163-166, 169, 170

water, 27, 28, 57, 62, 66, 68-71, 85, 120, 121, 137-140

wind, 5, 8, 27, 30, 51, 52, 56-58, 60-64, 68, 70, 72, 73, 75, 79, 80, 83, 84, 86, 99, 106, 114, 119, 139, 156, 158, 159, 162

window, 19, 51, 52, 54-56, 60, 61, 63, 69, 70, 99, 100, 165, 169

wine, 27, 28, 62, 70, 71, 82, 136

A Cure Of The Mind: The Poetics of Wallace Stevens
Theodore Sampson

In this compelling contribution to the study of Stevens' verse Dr. Theodore Sampson, Professor of American Literature at the University of Athens examines the world of Wallace Stevens as projected in *Harmonium*. He takes upon himself the daunting task of making sense of the work of a poet whose desire is "to live in the world but outside existing conceptions of it," and who, as a poet, takes to "musing the obscure."

Of *A Cure of the Mind*, the *Wallace Stevens Journal* wrote:

Written with grace and lucidity...I found Sampson's book a well-argued, highly readable, and important contribution to the study of Stevens' complex rhetoric.

224 pages, bibliography, index
Paperback ISBN: 1-55164-148-8 $19.99
Hardcover ISBN: 1-55164-149-6 $48.99

Images And Words: Change and Chaos in American Culture
Ioannis K. Stavrianos

Images and Words, by Ioannis K. Stavrianos, Doctate of Philosophy in English Literature and Culture from the University of Athens, explores the underside of nineteenth century American culture by revealing the linguistic, artistic or photographic conventions used to convey certain underlying ideas about the real world.

Dorothea Lange's photographs, *Migrant Mother* and *Drought Victims From Oklahoma*; Walt Whitman's, *Leaves of Grass;* George Inness' paintings, *Delaware Water Gap* and *The Lackawanna Valley*; Ralph Waldo Emerson's philosophy; and Wallace Stevens' poetry; are considered in relation to the objective world and to social relevance. The author also looks at Gerald Graff's analytic work on the political consequences of literary criticism and at Howard Sankey's views on scientific realism.

155 pages, bibliography, index
Paperback ISBN: 1-55164-150-X $19.99
Hardcover ISBN: 1-55164-151-8 $48.99

BOOKS OF RELATED INTEREST BY

Aphra Behn, by George Woodcock
Beyond O.J., by Earl Ofari Hutchinson
Certainties and Doubts, by Anatol Rapoport
Every Life Is a Story, by Fred H. Knelman
Humorous Sceptic, by N.Anthony Bonaparte
Making Waves, by Jim Bohlen
Mind Abuse, by Rose Dyson
Murray Bookchin Reader, by Janet Biehl and Murray Bookchin
Nationalism and Culture, by Rudolf Rocker
Oscar Wilde, by George Woodcock
Perspectives on Power, by Noam Chomsky
Peter Kropotkin, by George Woodcock
Rethinking Camelot, by Noam Chomsky
Russian Literature, by Peter Kropotkin
Writers and Politics, by George Woodcock
Year 501, by Noam Chomsky

send for a free catalogue of all our titles
BLACK ROSE BOOKS
C.P. 1258, Succ. Place du Parc
Montréal, Québec
H3W 2R3 Canada
or visit our web site at: http://www.web.net/blackrosebooks

To order books in North America:
(phone) 1-800-565-9523 (fax) 1-800-221-9985
In the UK & Europe: (phone) 44(0)20 8986-4854
(fax) 44(0)20 8533-5821

Printed by the workers of
MARC VEILLEUX IMPRIMEUR INC.
Boucherville, Québec
for Black Rose Books Ltd.